The Wander Year

OTHER BOOKS BY MIKE MCINTYRE

The Wander Year:

One Couple's Journey Around the World

Mike McIntyre

ISBN-13: 978-1495213816
ISBN-10: 1495213811

Publishing History
eBook edition / July 2011
CreateSpace paperback edition / February 2014

Cover illustration by Chuwy.

To get an email alert when Mike McIntyre's next book is released, sign up here: http://eepurl.com/Jl_gn

CONTENTS

A NOTE TO READERS

In January 2000, my longtime girlfriend, Andrea, and I departed on a yearlong journey around the world. We were in our early 40s and wanted to take a break from our routines. We rented out our San Diego house—furniture and pets included—and flew off.

Before we left, the *Los Angeles Times*, a publication I'd written for in the past, hired me to file a weekly column about our travels. We decided to call it "The Wander Year."

The travel editor's only request was to make the stories "really personal and really honest." She wanted to hear about squabbles, homesickness and food poisoning—as well as the many moments of wonder, adventure and awe.

This edition of "The Wander Year" contains everything that ran in the newspaper series, and more. Many of the columns have been expanded. (The original, shorter, series is available for purchase from the *Times* for about $200.)

Looking back on the odyssey, it's easy to recall how it started:

With a globe and an inflatable clothes hanger.

Part One:

Planning and Packing

Destination: The World

SAN DIEGO — There are two kinds of vagabonds: those who make room in their backpacks for an inflatable clothes hanger, and those who don't.

The around-the-world journey my girlfriend, Andrea, and I are about to start will feature members of both camps. Andrea deems the plastic blow-up device essential, whereas the first thing I plan to pack is a sense of humor. That's not to suggest there is nothing funny about an inflatable hanger. In fact, we may need to pull it out for a laugh should we succumb to dysentery in Kathmandu, say, or misplace our passports in a Saharan sand dune.

Our split over the best method of drying hand-washed attire is no small matter, as it may point to friction farther down the road. Sure, Andrea and I have been great friends for a dozen years, living together the last five. We have shared vacations in Ireland, France, Scotland, Guatemala and Ecuador without a single argument.

But prolonged travel through the cramped developing world—where we expect to be during much of our trip—is another animal entirely. Like a stint on a submarine, it tends to force all character flaws to the surface.

It's me I worry about, not Andrea. She is easygoing, bordering on serene. But before we clear U.S. Customs a year from now, I know I will somehow compel her to whack me upside the head with her inflatable hanger.

Our goal is to spend 2000 circling the globe, starting from our house in San Diego and heading west. We've penciled in an itinerary, but we're carrying a big eraser. No blueprints for this trip. We intend to pass through the South Pacific, Asia, the Indian subcontinent, Europe and North Africa, but we'll make most plans on the fly. Countries will be added, others dropped, and there's always a chance we'll end up somewhere we never considered, like Tierra del Fuego in South America.

If we sound a bit aimless, it's because we pretty much are. There is no grand purpose or point to our journey. The heaviest part of it, I suspect, will be our backpacks. We are not out to find ourselves, or even to lose ourselves. We're merely seeking a pause in our routines. Call it the Wander Year.

"I'm willing to take the risk, professionally," says Andrea, who is leaving a lucrative career. "I don't want to wait until I'm 65 to do the things I want to do. I may not live that long, and I may not want to do them then anyway. I just want a break."

Andrea is 40; I'm 42. Neither of us has been married, nor do we have children. That makes this next year less risky than it would be for many people. The $40,000 we've budgeted for the trip won't come out of a youngster's college fund. If ditching work during a booming economy proves a boneheaded move and we wind up flipping burgers into our 80s, we will have hurt only ourselves.

Andrea's most recent position was sales manager for the San Diego office of a major health insurance company. Her longest time off in 15 years of work was three weeks, and that was only once. Last month, after seven years of night school, she finished her master's degree in public health at San Diego State University. She figures she has earned a respite.

It's harder for me to rationalize my involvement in our year abroad. My résumé already includes a lengthy gap. In 1992 I jumped at a buyout offer from the *San Diego Union*, where I worked as a feature writer, when it merged with the *Tribune*. The buyout money allowed me to roam through Central America, Mexico and the U.S. for the next two years.

The danger of chucking a career to travel—which I have pointed out to Andrea—is that it's tough to return to the workaday world. I lasted four months in my next journalism job before despair led me to quit abruptly and hitchhike coast to coast with no money.

Crazy, I know, but I was lucky. I actually made a profit on my midlife crisis, turning the experience into a book called *The Kindness of Strangers: Penniless Across America*. A few years later, it's a new rut, but this time the demons I flee are far less melodramatic—prime-time television and Häaggen-Dazs ice cream.

We got the idea to travel for a year in December 1998, when another major insurance company bought Andrea's employer. There was a good chance her job would be eliminated and she would get a substantial severance package. Images of exotic destinations flashed in her head. Months later, when the sale went through, she was sad to learn she had a job with the new company. There would be no golden handshake.

But by then the fantasy had taken hold, and she decided to quit anyway.

Our initial plan was to take several trips over the course of a year, returning home between them. We concluded this was impractical since we needed to generate rental income from our house and it's hard to find tenants willing to sign a two-month lease. It made more sense to leave for a whole year.

Suddenly we went from studying individual pages in our atlas to spinning our globe. Andrea and I have traveled extensively throughout the Western Hemisphere and Europe, and we expect to go back to those parts of the world on future vacations. But one objective of this journey is to visit harder-to-reach countries, places that we may never have the chance to return to.

We quickly agreed on two destinations: Years ago, I grew fascinated with Vietnam after writing several articles on veterans of the war. Andrea countered with Bali, drawn by its rich culture and lush landscapes. It was a start.

Mapping the rest of our tentative route took much longer. We pored over dozens of travel books from the library, only to return them and check out dozens more. Neither of us had ever pondered New Zealand, but the more we read of its stunning beauty and friendly people, the surer we were we had to go. India and its teeming humanity soon became intriguing. While there, it seems prudent to venture into neighboring Nepal. We kept hearing from veteran travelers that Turkey was one of their favorite countries, so it was added. The current buzz surrounding Morocco is hard to resist. It will be impossible to skip Spain, where we each have visited several times. Fiji and Thailand easily made the list because two of our flights stop there.

Other countries still in the running include China, Myanmar (formerly Burma), Cambodia, Malaysia, Papua New Guinea, Australia, Croatia, Slovenia and Portugal. Oh, yes, and Kyrgyzstan. The Central Asian republic is tough to access, but I simply can't shake the image of cavorting with yaks and sleeping in yurts.

We are independent travelers, shunning organized tours and cruises. We enjoy temples and ruins as much as the next sightseer, but we are more enthralled by what we see between the sights. Serendipitous snapshots of life, honest and unrehearsed. Sudden glimpses of the sad and the sublime. We like the sensation of being on the way, in the middle, gone. It excites us to wake up in an unfamiliar place and greet the uncertainty of a new day.

After resolving to take the journey, there were ceaseless logistics to attend to. Our biggest concern was what to do with our pets. Maya is a smiling retriever-shepherd mix whose presence in our home has added years to the life of our aging cat, Aretha, a black American shorthair who had no previous exposure to aerobic activity. Saying goodbye to these two characters will be brutal.

We looked for someone to care for our pets in exchange for reduced rent. To our surprise, there was no shortage of candidates. We struck a deal with a friend of a friend, a responsible professional and animal lover. He's basically taking over our lives: furniture, plants, everything stays put. The utilities will stay in our name, and our tenant/pet sitter will pay the bills. The rest of our payments—credit cards, house, car, health insurance—will automatically be deducted from our checking account. We'll arrange to file our income tax returns and receive absentee voter ballots while away. Andrea updated her will. I thought of writing my first ever but decided against tempting fate.

The one colossal mistake we've made thus far is allowing four months to prepare for the trip: way too much time. I've traveled enough to know that the supreme reward of any journey—that rare and wondrous moment of epiphany—can't be planned. So why sweat the endless piddling details? I could have learned to play the ukulele in those four months.

Early on, I got sucked into the quicksand that is the World Wide Web. It seems every traveler has a home page filled with photos, advice and links to related sites. Before you know it, it's midnight and your eyes are bugging, but you can't release the mouse because that next link might have a nugget of information you think you desperately need. I knew that my pointing and clicking had gotten out of hand when it delivered me to a site titled "Fatal Events and Fatal Event Rates by Airline Since 1970." I'm an inquisitive guy, but there are some things I don't want to know.

We invested an absurd amount of time in a chart we dubbed the Weather Matrix. Down one side of a sheet of paper, we listed the countries we hope to visit. Across the top, we wrote the months of the year. We colored in the corresponding boxes: green for good weather, red for bad, yellow for tolerable. Routing the trip through the green zone creates an unorthodox itinerary. For example, the chart told us to travel to India after New Zealand, then double back to Indonesia. This adds hundreds of dollars to our airfare, but it's worth it to dodge monsoons and heat waves.

Given our modest budget, the sensible source for airline tickets was one of the agencies specializing in around-the-world fares. The three leading U.S. companies in the field—Air Brokers International, AirTreks and TicketPlanet—are based in San Francisco. Each can tack together a customized itinerary made up of deeply discounted one-way airfares on various well-known—and not-so-well-known—carriers. The resulting cost is often half of what you would pay by buying tickets directly from the airlines.

Global fares are advertised for as little as $995. But this is for travel in the low season, in one continuous direction, with stops in only a couple of popular cities, such as Bangkok and London. To zigzag, backtrack and dip into the Southern Hemisphere, as we intend to do, runs closer to $3,500 each. I spent countless hours playing at the Web site of AirTreks. Their page features a nifty interactive device called "TripPlanner" that allows you to create millions of custom itineraries and instantly get the estimated fares. But in the end we went with Air Brokers International because it was the quickest to respond to each of my phone calls, taking hours instead of days.

Our trip extends beyond the time most airlines sell seats to discounters, so we're leaving with only enough tickets to get us halfway around the world. We'll buy the rest in Bangkok, a mecca for cheap airfares.

The reactions of friends and relatives to our journey have ranged from envy to pity. My good friend Bruce, a chiropractor with a wife and two boys, played it down the middle when he said, "That is so far out of my realm." Most folks tell us we'll have a great time, but the look in their eyes fairly speaks, "Better you than me."

The most honest opinions of our world jaunt were conveyed by some of the Christmas presents we received. One friend gave us a first-aid kit, complete with an abdominal trauma bandage. Another bought us a travel clock equipped with a flashlight, smoke detector and intruder alarm. A third gave us the books *Come Back Alive* and *The Worst-Case Scenario Survival Handbook* (the latter contains tips on how to fend off a shark and elude a charging bull).

We're prepared to encounter a far deadlier creature—the mosquito—which is responsible for 1.5 million to 2.7 million deaths each year. While traveling through Asia, we'll take Lariam, an antimalarial drug that costs about $10 a pill. We're packing plenty of mosquito repellent and permethrin, an insecticide that is sprayed on clothing. We'll also carry a roll of adhesive tape to mend rips we may spot in hotel mosquito nets.

We switched our health coverage to a high-deductible plan with Blue Shield because it does not limit the length of time members may travel outside the country. Other health precautions include vaccinations for typhoid and hepatitis A. We'll also take iodine tablets to purify water wherever the bottled variety is unavailable.

When I told my doctor I was hitting the road for a year, he shot me a look of disbelief. Or maybe it was contempt. His longest vacation over the last 14 years was a single week. I felt more than a twinge of guilt on the drive home.

"Do you think we're being frivolous?" I asked Andrea.

"No," she said. "The point of life is to have fun."

I sometimes need to be reminded of the obvious.

Our budget took a huge hit before we even boarded our first flight. So far we've blown about $5,000 on equipment, clothes, footwear, health products, visas and guidebooks. Throw in the estimated $7,000 we'll spend on air fare, and we're down to making our way around the world on roughly $75 a day. That's a handsome sum in Southeast Asia but a pittance in Europe. We're banking on it all balancing out in the end.

Our first big expenditure was on his-and-hers internal-frame Eagle Creek backpacks—$285 apiece. The shoulder straps and hip belts stow into zippered compartments, allowing you to check the packs like regular baggage. They are appropriate for the moderate trekking we've planned and will leave our hands free when we're moving through cities—better to fend off touts and pickpockets.

As our departure day looms, the pile of stuff we'll try to cram into our packs grows ever higher. Our purchases reflect all the expert advice: lightweight nylon pants, Gore-Tex rain shells, titanium mugs, sewing kit, drain plug (for washing clothes in sinks), super-absorbent pack towels, 8-inch umbrellas, padlocks…the list goes on. Individually, each of these items makes sense. Collectively, they add up to our own personal outlet store. When Andrea tossed a copy of *War and Peace* onto the pile, it hardly made a difference.

The decision to take a year off and travel the world, renting the house, selling one of the cars—it was all child's play compared with the awesome task that now stands before us: packing. When globe-trotting, you are what you carry. So we will spend the remaining days before we leave defining ourselves: Five pairs of underpants or four? Yes or no to the miniature pillows? And what of that confounded inflatable contraption of Andrea's? It's always the little things that hang you up.

Part Two:

The South Pacific

Watching Life Slip
From Pacific Standard to Fiji Time

LAUTOKA, Fiji — Andrea and I decided to start our trip around the world with a vacation.

The endless preparations for our yearlong tour had sapped us. We were not ready to face the rigors of shoestring travel—incomprehensible tongues, mystery meals, the sweaty press of humanity. We would eventually rally, but first we needed a place where heavy lifting amounted to a cold drink and a back issue of the *New Yorker*.

Fiji beckoned. The 800-island South Pacific nation offered pristine beaches, a pleasant climate and warm, English-speaking people. A first stop here would allow us to wade into the shallow end of the world journey pool.

But we nearly did not make it. Three hours before we were to leave home in San Diego, we had yet to pack. The mountain of clothing and gear piled atop our dining room table mocked our modest backpacks. At the last instant, we panicked and pulled out two more bags, haphazardly stuffing them until they threatened to burst. (Yes, Andrea's inflatable hanger made the cut.) We told ourselves we would shed the excess luggage in New Zealand, India or wherever our arms fall off from the weight of stupidity.

Our frenzied packing agitated the pets, who will stay with the man renting our house. Aretha, the cat, fled into the laundry room, refusing to come out and say goodbye. Maya, the dog, ran circles around our legs, barking in the direction of her leash. The farewell was made sadder by the sight of my golf clubs, already looking neglected and forlorn in a corner of my office.

A construction crew was tearing up the street in front of our house, replacing the water main, and we had been unable to use our driveway for days. We begged the foreman to let us park long enough to load our luggage, and he gave us five minutes. Andrea maneuvered our Explorer between a bulldozer and a steamroller, I flung our bags in the back and we sped off. Four months of planning came down to this messy getaway, closer to an evacuation than a departure.

Andrea's mother—she's storing our car—and grandmother dropped us off at the airport. We flew all night, lost a day to the International Date Line and landed in Nadi (pronounced nondy), on Fiji's main island of Viti Levu. We grabbed a cab and rode 12 miles north to Lautoka, the jumping-off point for the Yasawa Islands, where we would later travel by boat. The lush mountains and fields outside the taxi window were so green in the morning sun, it almost hurt the eyes to look. We passed a train rattling down a narrow-gauge track, hauling cars laden with stacks of sugar cane, the crop that accounts for 40% of Fiji's exports.

After checking into the spartan Cathay Hotel ($24 a night) we wandered along Vitogo Parade, Lautoka's palm-lined main boulevard. We were instantly struck by the dichotomy that is Fiji. Only half the population consists of indigenous Fijians. The rest are mostly Fiji Indians, descendants of laborers recruited by British colonialists to work the cane fields in the late 1800s. Today Fijians own nearly all the land, while Indians control the business sector.

The Fijian women we saw wore vibrant floral or batik-patterned full-length dresses. Striding the same sidewalks were Indian women wrapped in richly colored, delicate saris.

The Indians we encountered were reserved, while the natives were the most outgoing people we have ever met. Every Fijian we passed smiled broadly and said "Good morning" or *"Bula,"* the common Fijian greeting, which literally translates to "life." Some leaned into our path as they spoke, ensuring their salutations were received. Even Fijians across the street called out *"Bula,"* stretching the four letters into BOOOO-LAAAH. At first I was suspicious, fearing they wanted something from us. Then I realized I had grown so cynical that I forgot it is still considered bad manners in some parts of the world not to greet a passing stranger.

We ducked into a Fijian bakery and bought pineapple turnovers, still too hot to eat. We carried them and a copy of the *Fiji Times* to an outdoor Indian cafe, where we feasted on chicken fried rice and samosas. The newspaper, the food, the dessert and a couple of Cokes cost less than $3.

It was Saturday, and the colorful town market was bustling. We strolled down rows of stands, inspecting the fresh eggplant, okra, carrots and an array of other vegetables and fruits. The vendors displayed their produce in orderly piles. Tiny handwritten signs advertised each "heap"—be it bananas or peppers—for the equivalent of about 25 cents.

Back at our hotel, we sipped sodas on the second-story veranda. A rugby match was underway at nearby Churchill Park, and we followed it through the branches of a sprawling tree. It was a serious, professional game, but the lighthearted Fijian fans filled the stadium with uproarious laughter.

Soon the sounds of choir practice at the Methodist church down the road drifted through the window on the breeze. A waitress sang sweetly as she set the tables behind us. The laughter, the singing and the rain that began to fall blended into a beautiful noise.

We finished our drinks and fought the vacation-mode urge to pop up and do something else. We finally realized that for the next year we had to be nowhere other than where we were. We leaned back in our chairs and set our watches to Fiji time.

Kava and Companionship in Paradise

NANUYA LAILAI, Fiji — Our boat was 15 miles northwest of Fiji's main island of Viti Levu when the skipper, Sala Saucoko, tapped me on the knee.

"We are now in Bligh Water," he said.

It was in this part of the South Pacific, in 1789, that Capt. William Bligh and 18 others were chased by two Fijian war canoes. Bligh and his men, cast adrift days earlier by mutineers on the Bounty, pulled frantically on the oars of their longboat, narrowly escaping the savages.

Saucoko laughed at the image of the sailors fleeing his ancestors. "They were lucky," he said. "If they catch them, they eat them."

The Fijians long ago replaced cannibalism with tourism. On this day, Saucoko was ferrying us to the Gold Coast Inn, a budget resort on Nanuya Lailai, one of the Yasawa Islands. The place was too new for the guidebooks (we'd heard about it in a Viti Levu hotel lobby), so Andrea and I were taking our chances—though risking far less than had Bligh and his crew.

When the one-square-mile island appeared off the bow, we broke into wide grins. This was the Fiji of our daydreams, a picture-postcard vision. Separating the green mountainside and the dazzling blue water was a white strip of sand, fringed by a line of coconut palms arching like swans' necks over the beach.

The Gold Coast Inn is no Club Med, but we were enthralled by its primitive charm. The entire resort consists of six thatched bungalows, called *bures* (BOO-rays), and two outhouses. The lobby is a shady spot beneath a rain tree, the dining room is a picnic table in the sand and the cash drawer is a traveling cosmetics case.

Our *bure* was built of tree limbs, reeds and palm fronds. Its only furnishings were a double bed and a mosquito net. We fell asleep at night to the sound of waves lapping the shore. Each morning we woke to a sunrise that turned the Pacific Ocean the color of a flame. Paying $39 a day for two, including three meals, we felt as though we were stealing paradise.

Little distinction is made between the resort and the village that extends up the hillside. The 20 or so workers are related to the owner, Filo Saucoko, Sala's wife. They treated us more like family members than guests.

We shared the resort with 19 other travelers, mainly Europeans, mainly young. Most were like us, people who had set aside their routines to explore the world. Our yearlong itinerary impressed our fellow vagabonds, who believe all Americans squeeze their journeys into an annual two-week vacation.

Ben, an Irish veterinarian, and his wife, Liz, an English pediatric nurse, had been traveling on the cheap for close to two years: the U.S., Central America, South America, Antarctica. Someone they met in the Cook Islands recommended the Gold Coast Inn. Both in their early 30s, they were postponing all major decisions—children, careers, house.

"As soon as you decide, you close all the doors," Ben said. "I used to be a control freak, but now we're down to our last $1,500, and I've never been happier. It's good to get out of a rut. So many people hate their jobs, but they don't do anything about it."

Diana, an advertising executive from London, was nearing the end of a 16-month world tour. Her final stop is Phoenix, where she will reunite with a lover from an earlier leg of her journey. "I'll see him for ten days," she said, "though it's the nights I'm looking forward to."

Another British woman, Cerys, took a leave from her job as a career counselor to travel for six months. She landed on Nanuya Lailai six weeks ago. "I've just sort of stopped here, haven't I?" she said, smiling.

One day, after a lunch of Spam, stir-fried vegetables and rice, Andrea and I followed two dogs to the other side of the island. As we splashed through the shallow, 80-degree water, poisonous sea snakes darted out of our way. We rounded a rocky point and beheld a deserted white crescent of sand fronting a calm, clear bay. It was Blue Lagoon Beach, one of the shooting locations for the 1949 film *The Blue Lagoon*, starring Jean Simmons, as well as the 1980 remake with Brooke Shields.

We donned our snorkel gear and kicked toward the reef. I peered through my mask and saw that fish of every size and color surrounded us. Velvety royal blue starfish, looking like five-legged Beanie Babies, clung to the sun-dappled ocean floor. The coral resembled massive deer antlers. It was like swimming inside a Discovery Channel program.

On our final night on the island, our hosts prepared a feast in honor of Millie, an Englishwoman celebrating her 19th birthday. Chicken, fish and lamb were wrapped in palm leaves and baked in a *lovo*, an earthen oven. Children draped flowers around Millie's neck and crowned her with a tinsel wreath. A white cake appeared, and we all sang "Happy Birthday."

After dinner, several of us joined the locals for a few rounds of kava, the Fijian national drink. We sat in a circle, legs crossed, as a man measured into a cloth some powder ground from the dried root of a pepper plant. Again and again he wrung the cloth in a large wooden bowl of water. When offered a coconut shell full of the grog, the recipient claps once, says *"Bula"* (life), drains the kava and claps three more times. The beverage looks like muddy water and tastes about the same. It is nonalcoholic, though many Fijians get looped from its tranquilizing effect. All I felt after four "high tides" (full shells) was a numb tongue and an urge to visit the outhouse.

In the morning, we exchanged e-mail addresses with fellow travelers we had grown fond of during the previous three days. It was hard to leave them and our gracious hosts. A Fijian woman we had yet to meet hugged us on the beach and thanked us for coming. As our boat motored away from the shore, we looked back and saw the whole island waving goodbye. I recalled a verse from "Isa Lei," a traditional farewell song the villagers sang the night before:

Isa Lei, the purple shadows fall
Sad the morrow will dawn upon my sorrow
Oh forget not when you are far away
Precious moments from Fiji.

Fleeing Paradise:
Whirlwind Departure Puts New Spin On South Pacific Idyll

WAYA ISLAND, Fiji — We stayed in Fiji one day too long.

On our last night at the Octopus Resort, we were joined by an obnoxious guest. She blew in, messed the place up and dominated all conversation. Her name was Cyclone Jo.

Three days earlier, we had been delighted to arrive by boat at this tropical hideaway on the western edge of the Fijian archipelago. Our spacious *bure*, a thatch bungalow, was elegant compared with the one we had enjoyed the week before on the island of Nanuya Lailai. It faced a gleaming white beach and included a private outdoor bathroom, allowing us to shower under the warm sun. The queen bed's white linens were adorned with a pile of red hibiscus flowers, matching the color and pattern of the curtains fluttering in the four windows.

The meals of fresh fish and curried lamb were tasty. One evening, residents from the nearby village of Nalauwaki entertained us with traditional Fijian song and dance. The next morning, several of us hiked over a jungle ridge, past pigpens and a cemetery, to hear villagers fill the cheery Methodist church with their joyful voices.

It had all been so idyllic.

Then Jo barged ashore, that salty wench. She was carrying some heavy baggage—predatory winds, lashing rains, breakers like avalanches.

On the morning we were to depart, Andrea and I awoke and found the resort's motorboat sinking in the angry sea. The storm had snapped its mooring line, leaving the craft to founder on the coral barrier reef. We rushed to help workers try to pull the boat from the surf with ropes.

We played tug of war with the ocean for 90 minutes, our hands growing red and blistered. We dodged falling coconuts as they blew from swaying palms overhead. The boat took on more water with each pounding wave. Finally, a breaker burst through the bow and a section of plywood flapped from the frame like the sole of an old shoe. Unable to drag the boat an inch farther, we tied off the lines and let nature have its way.

We retreated to the resort's restaurant, now encircled by a rising pool of rainwater. I assumed a boat would not be coming for us, and we ordered lunch. Before I finished my tuna sandwich, a woman appeared in the doorway, soaked to the skin and rattled. She was just off the boat from Viti Levu, Fiji's main island. A routine 90-minute crossing had turned into a five-hour ordeal. Many of the passengers were sick. The boat was now anchored in the roiling bay, waiting for us to board for the return trip to the port of Nadi.

"Don't go, don't go," the woman implored. "I wouldn't go back right now for a million dollars."

Six guests were scheduled to leave: Andrea and I, a Danish couple and their 5-year-old son, and a University of Michigan student named Andy. Now that the resort's motorboat lay wrecked on the beach, the only way out to the dual-engine catamaran was in a small rubber raft. The absence of life jackets and paddles meant more room for our lunacy.

The raft had already made one semi-successful trip from catamaran to shore, losing only two passengers. One managed to climb back in; the other desperately swam through the surf to return to the boat.

When the resort manager said it was our turn, I told him we'd like to stay another night. "Impossible," he said. The arriving guests had taken all the bungalows. He ordered us into the raft. The Danes refused to go, electing to camp out in the storm. Andy, Andrea and I reluctantly stepped into the pathetic rubber vessel.

A rope 100 yards long hung between a palm tree and the railing at the stern of the bobbing catamaran. Two Fijian men stood in the raft and began pulling us along the rope across the churning sea. Andy and Andrea sat, while I crouched on all fours. Every time the catamaran lurched, the taut rope whacked the side of my face and neck.

"Sit down! Sit down!" Andrea kept yelling. I held my preposterous position, thinking it somehow more stable, as the rope continued to thrash my head.

I looked back at the beach and saw that many of the young European guests had braved the elements to offer us their support. At least that's what I thought they were doing until several of them whipped out cameras and started shooting. I could already hear the family slide show back in Berlin: "Look,

Uncle Wolfgang, here's a picture of the idiot Americans getting swept out to sea."

It was low tide, and the jagged coral ahead jutted from the surface like so many shark teeth. The Fijians waited for a surge of water to cover the reef, then pulled madly on the rope. They misjudged the timing and delivered us into the jaws of a mighty wave.

I caught a glimpse of Andy, who already had the look of a goner. Andrea smiled maniacally at the thundering breaker. Our handlers screamed something in Fijian. I tried to recall whether the evacuation provision of my health insurance policy also covered remains.

The crushing surf bucked the raft into the air, and for one terrifying instant it appeared we would be flung into the clutches of the reef. But when we came down, it was water, not coral, smacking the bottom of the raft.

Once we were on board the catamaran, Capt. Osea Namuatique proudly noted that his was the only boat to take on Cyclone Jo. All other skippers had obeyed the Marine Department order to stay in the harbor. He explained that the name of the catamaran, Dau Veivueti, is Fijian for "rescue boat." It was unclear whether he had risked all to rescue us or our money.

The return cruise was easy—as long as we ignored the howling gale, the horizontal rain and the whitecaps that resembled convulsing icebergs.

"Getting on that boat was the craziest thing I've ever done," Andy said. "Don't tell my mother."

Straying Into Hostel Territory
In New Zealand

AUCKLAND, New Zealand — We thought we had boarded the wrong flight in Fiji and returned to the U.S.

Parts of this hilly waterfront city look like San Francisco. The most prominent landmark, Sky Tower, evokes the Seattle Space Needle. And the America's Cup yacht races in Hauraki Gulf recall home, San Diego, where the last three Cups were contested.

Everything about Auckland seemed familiar, right down to ubiquitous Starbucks. So it was the last place we figured to experience culture shock.

It was not the culture of the native Maori that shocked us, nor that of the immigrant Polynesians. It was the culture of youth.

Upon arriving in New Zealand—the second stop on our world tour—we were distressed to discover we had mistakenly booked ourselves into a youth hostel. It was Andrea's fault. She had trusted me with the reservation.

I made the booking by phone before we left home, acting on our plan to confirm the first night's lodging in each new country. The name of the place—International Backpackers—

should have clued us that this was not the ideal accommodation for a couple in their 40s. But the guidebook said it was in the "stylish" Parnell district and mentioned "double rooms"—a term that to me conjures a king bed, cable TV and coffee maker.

The first hint that we had strayed from our comfort zone was the puzzled expression of the girlish desk clerk when I asked about our private bathroom. She said in a whisper that we could use the common bathroom at the end of the hall. We were too stunned to flee, so I paid the nightly double rate of $23, plus a $5 key deposit.

Carrying luggage from our rented Toyota Corolla into the industrial brick building reminded me of moving into my college dorm. The bulletin board was covered with notices for rides and part-time jobs. Reggae music pumped from behind a closed door. The sweet smell of cannabis hung in the air. All that was missing was a study lounge.

Our shock was reflected in the fresh faces of the other lodgers. We were all travelers, but the similarities ended there. I was fairly certain Andrea and I were the only guests without bleached hair, tattoos or nose rings. And although we had recently dropped out, they looked as though they had recently dropped out of high school. For the first time in my life, I felt in danger of being called "Pops."

We hurried down the hall, passing dormitories crammed with bunk beds. At least we don't have to sleep in one of those, I thought, turning the key to our double room. But when the door opened, there they were: his-and-hers stacked twin beds.

The bunks nearly filled the cell-like room, illuminated by a hanging bare bulb.

"I get the top one," I said.

Andrea slumped on the bottom bunk, the foam mattress sinking through the wooden slats.

"*Miiiiiike,*" she groaned. "We're too old to be staying in a youth hostel. It's embarrassing."

I escaped into a daydream of my first and only hosteling trip. Europe, 1978. I wistfully recalled Susan, a comely California girl I had met in an Amsterdam hostel. My reverie burst when I realized she was now old enough to be the mother of the guitar player next door, who kept mangling the opening notes from "Layla."

I ventured out to inspect the facilities. They were exactly like those I'd encountered 22 years ago: mildewy shower clogged with hair, sink stopped with tissue, hand towel as sheer as a veil.

When Andrea summoned the courage to step into the hall, she was relieved to see we weren't the oldest guests. Coming down the corridor was a balding man. But as he drew near, he turned out to be a younger fellow suffering premature hair loss. Andrea quickly ducked into the bathroom before creeping back to our room.

"What are we doing here?" we each said again and again. In the parlance of our generation, we were freaking out.

The bunks each came with only one sheet, so we broke out the silk sleep sacks we'd packed for the grungy beds we didn't expect to see until later in the trip. Andrea slept little after two cats climbed through the window and joined her in bed. She didn't shoo them, afraid they might object.

When the cats left in the morning, we hit the street, looking for less ludicrous lodging. We landed at the quaint Parnell Inn, where we felt neither foolish nor flabby.

We dined that evening at SPQR, a trendy bistro in the posh Ponsonby neighborhood, west of the city center. It was an overreaction to the hostel. Andrea had the rib-eye steak on a bed of spinach, with portobello mushrooms and potatoes pan roasted with rosemary, all in a red wine sauce. I had the free-range sautéed chicken marinated in garlic, accompanied by a fresh green salad with goat cheese. Drinks, dinner, desert and tip came to $39. It's hard to spend more for a meal in New Zealand, where travel expenses run about half of those in America.

It had been a day of extremes. I started it in a bunk bed and ended it behind a plate of profiteroles dripping with coffee crème anglaise. I wondered what they were eating in the communal kitchen back at the hostel.

Adventures in Paradise…
No, Make That Parasites

NELSON, New Zealand — A traveler's riddle:

Question: What do you get when you cross three meals a day with food handlers who lack soap and hot water?

Answer: Sick.

I guess I picked something up in Fiji other than seashells. The culprit may have been the *lovo*, the earthen oven feast where villagers put fish and fowl onto our plates with their bare hands. Or it may have been the kava, the ceremonial drink made by a man who submerges his hands into the communal bowl.

Either way, I confused paradise with parasites.

The symptoms struck the day we arrived in New Zealand, where I soon felt lower than a pregnant sheep dog's belly. My insides gurgled like a chemical factory. Then came fever, sweats and chills. Within a week, most of my sightseeing was restricted to the bathroom. When I did step out, it was with a stomach-distress bag and directions to the nearest loo.

New Zealand is a great place to be sick, actually. It's clean, convenient and comfortable. Motel units with kitchens go for $40 a night and come with milk in the fridge. In Wellington, the capital, our room at the Wellingtonian was almost like an apartment, equipped with a washer-dryer and a stereo.

"It's almost like home," I said to Andrea as she cooked dinner and I channel-surfed from the bed.

"There's a few things missing," she said. "But if you mean I'm working while you're watching TV, you're right."

Each day, we traveled shorter distances between hotels, as I sought the security that comes with porcelain. I stopped eating, unable to keep anything down. I grew so weak that I could no longer muster the energy to criticize Andrea's driving—tailgating, fish-tailing around mountain curves, driving on the right (in a country where they drive on the left).

We loaded our rental car onto a ferry and crossed Cook Strait to the South Island. When we reached Nelson, a mellow city on Tasman Bay, I could go no farther. Andrea checked us into the Mid City Motor Lodge and called the local hospital for a referral.

I sensed that the Kiwi approach to health care is more casual than others when I rang Dr. Gill Harker's office for an appointment. Playing in the background was the unmistakable wail of the Rolling Stones' "Gimme Shelter." When I staggered into the office, I was extended a "G'day" by a receptionist dressed in a tank top and gym shorts. Harker greeted me in jeans and Teva sandals. The music now thumping from her office boombox was Led Zeppelin's "Trampled Under Foot."

Harker led me to an examination room, where I half-expected her to say "Take two classic rock CDs and call me in the morning." But apart from the thermometer under my arm, her methods were conventional. She poked and prodded and quickly found my problem: an enlarged, tender liver.

She directed me to the medical lab, where all the usual suspects—along with specimens that I had never given—were wrangled from my body. I tested negative for hepatitis and giardia, but my liver function test registered four times above the normal range.

Harker diagnosed me with a viral liver infection, most likely of Fijian origin. She said I'd feel "washed out" for several weeks and commanded me to bed. There was no cure. I could only ride this sucker out.

Things got worse before they got better. I became more familiar with New Zealand tile work; the rest of the time I was on my back. Andrea drifted in and out of my daze. One day our entire interaction was the following exchange:

"Do you want me to take your shoes off now?" she asked.

"No thanks," I said. "I need something to look forward to."

Harker prescribed anti-nausea pills so I could eat some broth and yogurt. With nourishment came strength and a desire to return to the road. At the end of the week, the doctor pronounced me in fine color and released me from her care, with the agreement that I undergo another blood test before I left the country. (Later lab worked confirmed that my liver was returning to normal.)

My treatment cemented New Zealand as the bargain destination of the developed world. Three visits with Harker, two batteries of lab tests and two prescriptions came to $51.

But I paid in other ways. I started the trip weighing 192 pounds; I was now down to 155. My legs resembled two knobby noodles. And my pants now hung halfway down my backside, making me look like an aging skateboarder.

What's more, I felt guilty about derailing the trip. My illness forced us to cancel two backpacking treks, and we'd seen much less of the country than we planned.

"This hasn't been so bad," Andrea said of the downtime. "It just feels so good not to be working."

One of the many things I love about Andrea is that she is easily pleased. Her unemployed and me sick, and our world journey is complete.

New Zealand's Clean, Green Tedium Machine

FRANZ JOSEF, New Zealand — New Zealand is the centerfold of the World Atlas. Smokin' hot. Sexy. A 10.

But it has no edge. It lacks that tiny scar or birthmark that builds character. It's like a beauty queen—gorgeous but dull.

This is not a problem for the short-term sightseer. But travel the country for five weeks, as we're doing, and the ceaseless beauty becomes a beast.

New Zealand is so breathtaking you could suffocate. As we drove south from Auckland, each bend of the road revealed a vista that elicited an oooh and an aaah. Now, 2,000 miles later, it's ugh, not another rain forest, not another snowcapped peak, not another waterfall.

Even the rhododendron-lined motorways demand to be photographed.

"I can't take any more scenery," Andrea said during a long day of nonstop clean and green.

Traveling in New Zealand is like eating in a restaurant that serves only dessert. After your umpteenth chocolate mousse, you start craving lima beans. Each day, we push back from nature's table, stuffed, unable to consume any more sights.

And Mother Nature scolds: "Finish your scenery. Don't you know there are tourists starving for scenery in Belarus?"

Physical perfection looks great on a supermodel, but it glazes the eyes when draped over a 104,000-square-mile country. We yearn for a pimple on the landscape. Nothing too severe. No toxic waste dump or open-pit mine. A cigarette butt, perhaps, a gum wrapper, anything to relieve the monotonous natural wonders.

We are trapped inside a postcard, and we are not alone. It is the high season, summer Down Under, and everyone is here, delivered by Lonely Planet to this not-so-lonely corner of the world. We all circle the island nation like baggage on a carousel, engaged each night in a game of musical hotels.

Kiwis raise sheep, but they cultivate tourists. Government road signs announce every upcoming B&B and cafe. Tiny towns without service stations are sure to have visitor centers wallpapered with brochures. You may run out of gas, but you'll have plenty to read when you do.

Pretty hamlets transform into parking lots. Tourist buses, camper vans and rental cars vie for patches of asphalt as cyclists and hitchhikers pick their way through the pileup. Overhead, whirlybirds whisk shutterbugs to loftier sights.

Some of the hiking trails are so packed that we shuffle along like a chain gang. The steady flow of oncoming traffic prompts me to vary my greetings, like a flight attendant greeting boarding passengers: "Hi," "Hello," "Howdy." Then my voice goes hoarse, and I get by with a nod.

At Tongariro National Park on the North Island, we hiked the Tongariro Crossing, a 10 1/2-mile trek billed as "the finest one-day walk in New Zealand." The climb took us past volcanoes, craters and emerald lakes. The view was spectacular—for the few brief moments I could see around the ascending path of rumps.

By the time Andrea and I arrived here in Franz Josef, on the west coast of the South Island, we were ready to form a tourists' union and declare a strike. Instead, we each paid $19.50 to walk on some ice.

The Franz Josef Glacier, like the nearby Fox Glacier, is one of the world's few warm-weather glaciers. Storms from the Tasman Sea dump huge amounts of snow in the coastal Southern Alps. The resulting ice pack descends the steep valley at a rapid rate—up to 21 feet a day—allowing it to tumble nearly to the beach. Picture a river of ice flowing down Topanga Canyon and you have the idea. That said, we still felt like passengers on a busy theme park ride as the shuttle bus approached the attraction.

But once I laced up my rented ice boots and stepped on the glacier, something strange happened. The glacier spoke to me.

"Forget the 500 other tourists around you," the glacier said. "Forget the guides and their tired jokes. Forget the helicopters hovering above. Forget all that and just look at me."

And I did.

And it was awesome.

A mountain of ice had melted my heart. I was shocked by my own surprise. How did something so magnificent sneak up on me?

OK, New Zealand, I'll love you.

Part Three:

Asia

Caught in the Grip of Delhi Delirium

NEW DELHI — We boarded a jet in New Zealand and stepped off a spaceship in India. It's not a small world, after all.

That's no slam on this alien place. We are happy our journey has taken a turn for the weird. We have come to embrace the madness.

We landed after dark at Indira Gandhi International Airport, where I almost fell over a wheelbarrow of sand parked just inside the arrival gate. I recovered in time to sidestep a black hole where an escalator used to be.

A fellow traveler told us the trick to enjoying India is to laugh when you want to scream. So I guffawed uproariously when the immigration official inexplicably closed his booth just as Andrea and I had reached the front of the line.

While awaiting our turn at another booth, I read up on the scams Delhi cabdrivers pull on tourists. Some insist the hotel you booked is full. Others claim the road there is closed. The craftier ones are flagged down by cohorts disguised as cops, who warn of rioting ahead. The objective is to steer you to a different, costlier hotel, where your cabbie gets a kickback.

We bought a prepaid taxi voucher inside the airport, at least taking the meter out of play. So I was impressed when 15 men lurking outside nevertheless managed to insert themselves into a transaction that had already been negotiated.

The man who snatched the voucher from my hand turned out not to be the driver, but the driver's brother. He promised to introduce us—just as soon as we ran the gantlet of his buddies. Hands reached through the dark to relieve us of our bags. Men pressed close, yammering in our faces. I fumbled through my pockets for the hotel address, fearing my money, credit card and passport were dropping to the ground.

As the pack closed tighter, I wanted to fling a fistful of *rupees* in the air and flee. At last, a policeman stepped in and uttered a few words of Hindi, and the human noose unknotted. All we needed to do now was expel a man who tried to jump into our cab with us, and we were off.

It's a mistake to arrive in a poor country at night, jet lagged and disoriented. My usual paranoia was amplified by the week's dose of Lariam, an anti-malaria drug that sets me on teeth-gnashing edge. I wished there were some way to convey this to our cabbie, who must have wondered why I clutched my pen like a knife.

I opened my door while we were moving to make sure we weren't locked in. I urged Andrea to do the same, and she looked at me as if I were a lunatic. Andrea expects the best from strangers, and I expect the worst. That way one of us is never disappointed.

Our cabbie professed ignorance of our hotel's location, Paharganj, even though it is a well-known tourist area near the train station. He stopped at other hotels, insisting I go in to "get directions." I figured this was a ploy for commissions and told him to keep driving.

The long ride allowed us to study Indian traffic laws. Near as I can tell, there are none. Cars, auto-rickshaws, cycle-rickshaws and cyclists speed along, fender to thigh. They stay close enough to read the "Keep Distance" sign on the bumper in front. It's tempting to say the chaotic flow somehow works, but it doesn't. During our first 24 hours in India, seven people were killed in New Delhi traffic accidents—an average day.

I had booked a room at the Hotel Syal over the Internet, spending $28 per night, no small sum in India. (Budget accommodation in the $5 to $10 range is plentiful.) But my faith in e-commerce was shattered when our room did not match the pretty pictures on the Web site.

The door to Room 408 opened to a rectangle of squalor. The carpet was ripped and greasy. The bed had one sheet, which looked as if it hadn't been changed since the British Raj. The rust-colored crushed velvet headboard shone with grime. The sink was growing a beard.

"I can't believe how filthy these walls are," Andrea said. "How could they get so dirty?"

We laughed and laughed—until we realized this might be our cleanest room in India.

I peered out the tiny barred window at what looked like a construction site engulfed in flames. It turned out to be a multi-story jumble of concrete and corrugated metal shacks, each of them missing a wall or roof. Families cooked over open-air fires in the dark. The hovels were linked by a series of makeshift stairs and ladders. Like those in an M.C. Escher drawing, the steps appeared to lead everywhere—and nowhere.

In the lobby the next morning, Western guests chuckled nervously about a Canadian backpacker who arrived at the hotel earlier in the week to begin his four-month tour of India. The young man was so unhinged by what he saw on the ride from the airport, he was afraid to go outside. The next day, he flew back to Vancouver.

When we walked out into the street, I was reminded of a Russian proverb: To see once is better than to hear a thousand times. None of the tales we'd heard of India could have adequately prepared us for what now unfolded before our eyes.

Funneling along a road no wider than a car were all manner of people, animals and machines. Cows lumbered beside us, oblivious to the incessant honking of the scooters and rickshaws weaving through the throng. Fingerless beggars extended their stumps to us as we tiptoed over dung and dead rats. Dogs with more character than hair pawed at piles of rubbish. Men squatted against walls to defecate. A girl arched her back, grabbed her ankles and rolled down the mucky street like a tire.

The scene was like a giant, busy mural. You could never stand back far enough to take it all in. You have to view it in pieces.

Andrea stepped into a mud puddle. At least she hoped it was mud.

"Serves you right for bringing a $300 pair of Mephistos to India," I cracked.

Suddenly there was a baby girl at our feet, fallen from her mother's arms. In an instant, the wheel of a cycle-rickshaw was nearly upon her. By the time the scream traveled from the mother's mouth to the rickshaw driver's ear, the weight of the rickshaw and its three adult passengers had come to rest atop the infant's legs.

After the rickshaw continued over the baby, the mother swept the girl up off the street. The baby opened her mouth to cry, but nothing came out. The mother blew into the baby's mouth and rushed her into a vendor's stall, and the rickshaw driver pedaled away.

Before we could comprehend what we had just witnessed, a blond monkey came running down the road, and a pigeon crapped on our shoulders.

I must have a sixth sense because it feels like more than five have been assaulted.

India's Essence: Peacocks Amid Pigeons

JAIPUR, India — The peacock we glimpsed from our hotel window glided through pigeons atop an unfinished building with rusty reinforcement rods spiking a polluted sky.

The elegant, exotic and enchanting amid the annoying, drab and dirty. That's India.

As we journey into the northwestern state of Rajasthan, we seek India's figurative peacocks. But many days they elude us, and we are left choking on pigeon feathers.

Flocks of vendors, touts and rickshaw drivers flutter and flap about us, warbling their relentless pitches:

"From which country?"

"Just looking is OK."

"Rickshaw! Rickshaw!"

"Why are Westerners so unfriendly?"

"Hello" is rarely a simple greeting but an invitation to an exasperating entanglement. Politeness is a sign of weakness. A dozen "No, thank you's" give birth to a dozen more. The only way out is to ignore the man in your face or shout at him. Not much of a choice.

We were only five minutes in Pushkar, on the shore of the sacred Pushkar Lake, before I told Andrea they should rename the place Pushykar. The obnoxious vendors were outdone by bands of phony Hindu priests, who smile and press flowers into the palms of tourists.

"Throw in lake," they say. "Make a wish. Holy lake." Fall for the come-on and on the steps leading to the lake you're hit up for a "donation" to the Hindu god Brahma. Decline the flower, and smiles turn to snarls as the "priests" chase you down the street cawing: "You must! You must!" After this, the honesty of the beggar lepers seems refreshing.

Here in Jaipur, the capital of Rajasthan, walking is an extreme sport. Crossing the road, we froze in a raging river of traffic.

"This is total chaos," Andrea said, laughing.

An endless flow of buses, scooters and auto-rickshaws rushed past. Move an inch left and a motorcycle handlebar catches you in the gut. An inch right, your foot becomes a speed bump. And mind the horns of the bull moseying up behind you.

Where is the payoff? we wondered. Where is the peacock?

The elephant, its trunk painted yellow and blue, heralded the coming magic. We rounded its great gray rear, stepped through an arched gate and entered the old walled city. Here the peacock in India opened its brilliant plumage, knocking all the pigeons from our path.

We wandered through the bustling bazaar, if not undetected, at least unmolested. Jaipur exploded in a rainbow riot of color. The terra-cotta buildings and their green shutters glowed in the setting sun. Women in saris of citrus colors—lemon, lime, orange—eased by spice shops, dodging vegetable carts pulled by camels.

We marveled at the commerce conducted in the smallest of spaces. A mechanic sat on the ground rebuilding a motorcycle engine in the shade of a goat. A barber stepped out of his tiny stall to shave the right side of his customer's face. Barber's straight razor to customer's neck, cow's nose to barber's elbow—everything managed to fit.

The spectacle at eye level was so captivating that it took a while to notice the monkeys overhead. Scores scrambled along the verandas, some jumping into a tree. A mother and infant peeled bananas for Andrea's camera while a man with two right thumbs stopped to tell me the monkey's place in Indian culture. The monkey god Hanuman is a hero of the Hindu legend Ramayana, the man said, so monkeys are given refuge across India.

My view of the monkeys was suddenly obscured by a box containing a battery-operated fan, pushed into my face by a vendor who now squawked broken English in my ear: "Four hundred rupees only! Technical defect, one year's guarantee!" *Can't he see the magnificent monkeys?* I wondered. And he probably wondered in turn: *Can't he see the magnificent machine?* One man's magic is another's menace.

We ambled past the flower stands, where we met Sonu—cycle-rickshaw wallah, prince of the city and pure peacock. As the other rickshaw drivers crowded and crowed, Sonu reclined on his bicycle, smiling broadly, knowing we would pick him.

"I will teach you a Hindi word," he said. "*Chello*. It means *go*. In India, you will use this word a lot."

"*Chello*," he snapped at the gaggle of competitors, shooing them with a dismissive wave.

He turned back to us. "Hello, *chello*," he said, smiling. "Hi, bye. A little joke."

We hired Sonu, but he did not set a fare. We could pay him what we liked, he said. Sure, he would take us for a ride, but we'd be riding in a peacock-drawn carriage.

As he pedaled us through the old pink city, he rang the bell of his bike, shouted mirthful greetings to passersby and shared some of his life's story. He is 18, one of four children. His father "sells little things you put in your mouth." (We think he means peanuts.) He bought his cycle-rickshaw with $130 borrowed from his girlfriend. When he earns enough to pay her back, he'll marry her.

"No money, no honey," he said. "No wife, no life."

Outside our hotel, Sonu gently persuaded us to part with $3 for his services. It was 10 times the going rate, but the rare bird catches the rare price.

It was dark, and the little flashlight in my pocket had somehow engaged and was now shining through my pants. When I pulled it out to turn it off, Sonu beamed.

"If you give me the light, I will never forget you," he said.

In a country of 1 billion people, I figured I needed at least one friend. So I removed the light from my key ring and handed it to Sonu.

"Don't forget me," I called after him as he pedaled off. But he had already vanished into a flock of pigeons.

India's Rule of the Road: Just Cringe

AGRA, India — There are millions of deities worshiped in India. I didn't know the name of the icon mounted on the dash of our driver Bhanwar Singh's car, but when we pulled out to overtake the bus in front of us, I prayed it was the God Who Protects Those Who Pass on Blind Curves.

The truck rumbling at us when we came out of the turn was as big as a barn and growing by the instant. The truck driver honked. The bus driver honked. Our driver honked. Nobody braked.

Singh yanked the wheel, aiming the car for the narrowing gap between the two hulking vehicles. We slipped through with only enough spare room for a ray of hope.

It was Day 1 of a 13-day road trip around northwestern India, and our nerves were already as fried as old spark plugs. The 1,200-mile journey took Andrea and me west to Jaisalmer, near the border of Pakistan, before looping east to Agra, where we toured the Taj Mahal. We logged most of the miles in Rajasthan, a desert state studded with forts, palaces and temples.

In Pushkar, where we started, we approached a hotel travel director to ask about train schedules. Ten minutes later, he had our names on a contract for one of the hotel's Ambassadors—

the ubiquitous Indian-made auto that is a cross between a London taxi and a Volkswagen Beetle—complete with a non-English-speaking driver.

Hiring a car and driver at $26 a day, including gas, cost little more than train tickets for two to our planned destinations, the agent said. Plus, we would have local transportation at every stop on our itinerary. What he didn't disclose was that we would feel like stunt doubles in the chase sequence of a B-grade Indian action film.

Driving in India is anarchy. The concepts of right-of-way and traffic lanes are nonexistent. Asphalt, like air, belongs to everyone.

A road scarcely wider than two cars often holds a taxi, rickshaw, bus, lorry, scooter and camel cart, all hurtling to the blinking point in a huge game of chicken. A happy consequence of this style is that in a country where everyone drives like a lunatic, there is no place for road rage. Everybody merrily careens toward impending carnage.

A hotelier tried to persuade us there was a method to the madness. "American drivers watch out for the rules," he said. "Indian drivers watch out for each other." It made sense, in theory, until we rolled by the first of many crumpled metal carcasses littering the landscape, abruptly buried in the sand by drivers whose dashboard deities had failed them.

In relative terms, Singh was an excellent driver, and he had the documentation to prove it. Swerving around cows and pedestrians, he handed us a guest book signed by previous clients. "He was extremely capable and agile in dodging huge trucks," noted Nadia and Doug of the U.S. Jon and Nick from

England wrote, "Thanks for a scary ride!" In no time, our sole objective was to add our names to the list of satisfied survivors.

There were moments when that goal seemed too ambitious, as I suddenly grasped the appeal of the Hindu belief in reincarnation. Singh, a former tank driver in the Indian Army, operated the vehicle as if a giant gun on the hood could obliterate all obstacles in our path. His passing technique was so precise, I could see my horrified expression reflected in the chrome bumpers of onrushing trucks.

When not covering my eyes, I tried to distract myself with the view out the passenger window. Much of Rajasthan is dull and brown, yet it teems with life. Water buffalo, deer and monkeys are rarely out of sight. It was like driving through a zoo with no cages.

One day, a herd of blue bulls—ox-sized antelopes— thundered across the road. Even Singh was surprised, and for once he was forced to use the brakes.

On the long stretches between cities, the dung-plastered mud walls of the goatherds' huts baked in the hot sun. Women balanced clay jugs of water atop their heads, their colorful saris billowing in the desert wind. Little boys stood on the roadside, blowing us kisses as we flew by.

South of Bikaner, a mob blocked the road and demanded a "toll." Young men yelled at us and pounded on the car. Singh looked rattled by the shakedown, but I felt relieved. At least we weren't moving.

When we doubled back to the crowded region of north central India, there were more vehicles, animals and people to pass or dodge. Close calls got closer, near misses got nearer as

Singh tapped out a nonstop tune on his horn. I grew more frightened and frayed. When I went to bite my nails, I saw they were perspiring.

Before we left Pushkar, I had asked the travel agent the appropriate tip for a driver in India. "Whatever is in your heart," he said. So when Singh dropped us at the Agra train station, I looked into my heart and wondered: What price do you put on abject terror, fear and trauma?

Fifty bucks seemed right. Singh, whose monthly salary is about the same, looked pleased.

When we boarded the overnight train that would take us east, a drunken man was drooling and babbling in our sleeping compartment. It was the conductor.

I missed Singh already.

Taking Stock
As a Passage to India Ends

NEW DELHI, India — I wake up with one nerve, and India is on it.

Time to lace up our wandering shoes, I tell Andrea. She offers no resistance, and we're packed in five minutes.

We try to flee Varanasi, the sacred city on the Ganges River, but every train out for the next week is booked. I panic and, without consulting Andrea, blow $160 on two plane tickets. These only get us here to the capital, where we learn all flights to Nepal are full.

The thought of spending another day in this country causes me to hyperventilate. I spot a sign for Turkmenistan Airlines and wonder what the weather is like in Ashgabat this time of year. I fear that the wheels have come completely off my rickshaw.

Will the wander year become the squander year? It's too soon to tell. But mistakes have been made.

A progress report on our journey thus far:

Luggage: Lug it here, lug it there; now we know why it's called luggage. Poor packing forced us to depart with two bags too many. San Diego friends John and Lauren flew to our rescue in New Zealand, carrying home one of the extra suitcases after we all hiked the celebrated Milford Track.

We're now down to one piece of luggage besides our backpacks, but it's the size of a body bag. The pathetic part is that it doesn't contain a thing we can't buy along the way. The heaviest items—our year's supply of guidebooks—are available at every other corner shop. Likewise the extra shampoo, deodorant, sunscreen and flashlight batteries we're carting around the world.

Whoever said to pack half as much stuff and take twice as much money had it right. I dumped a dozen spiral notebooks several hotel rooms ago when I realized countries other than the U.S. made paper.

Funds: We're way over our original budget of $75 a day, thanks mainly to New Zealand. That country is such a bargain, it's easy to get seduced into a higher class of travel. In Queenstown, for example, we passed on comfortable $30 motel rooms in favor of a three-story lake-view townhouse we rented for a week at $65 a night.

If we were ever traveling on a shoestring, it belonged to a knee-high boot. What Andrea calls "good value" now guides our food, lodging and transportation choices. As she rightly points out, we don't ride Greyhound at home, so why take chicken buses in the developing world? Some days, a few dollars spells the difference between enjoying a place and merely tolerating it. Yet no amount of money could buy us a decent night's rest in India, where the mattresses are as thin as my patience.

Clothes: If I have one strength as a world traveler, it is my minimalist approach to fashion. I'm down to four pairs of boxers, and I'm contemplating cutting that number in half. Andrea won't divulge how many pairs of underpants she's carrying, but her pack looks like the sale bin at a Nordstrom Rack. She gets on me for wearing the same shirt 11 days in a row, suggesting I mix things up for her benefit. I counter that I don't want to have both my shirts dirty at once.

I now admit that the inflatable clothes hanger I chided Andrea for packing is a brilliant device. Most hotel rooms we occupy lack closets or even a chair to drape clothes over. Many days I jealously observe one of Andrea's hand-washed articles airing on the plastic blowup hanger while my laundry dries on a filthy windowsill.

Spirits: It can't be fun for Andrea to watch a 42-year-old man prancing in his underwear, singing songs from the rockumentary *This Is Spinal Tap*, but she never complains about my morning routine. Being together 24/7 would be tough at home, let alone while roaming from hotel to hotel, country to country. But we've yet to exchange a harsh word. Apart from being well matched, I think we both know that the minute we turn on each other, the journey gets poisoned.

There are days like today when we would rather be elsewhere—St. Andrews, Scotland, say, or Telluride, Colorado—but there are none when we regret taking this year off. We sometimes fret that the trip has yet to be defined. We are in transition—no longer tourists but not quite travelers. Nothing feels easy. Then again, we're seeing the world. How hard can that be?

We are lucky, and we know it. We occasionally go to bed stressed, but we always wake up grateful. Well, almost always.

Spirits Rise
Amid Comforts of Kathmandu

KATHMANDU, Nepal — In one of the stranger quirks of the world time zone map, Nepal is 15 minutes ahead of neighboring India. But it feels like a light-year.

Hotel beds here come with two sheets—both clean. Street vendors don't treat sales as a blood sport. And waiters don't hand you your fork by the tines.

"Pinch me and make sure I'm not dreaming," I tell Andrea.

India, as it turns out, is not for everyone—just a billion people.

We have flown to tiny Nepal to recover and recuperate. If we get ambitious, we may even relax.

We arrive feeling more like refugees than travelers. The hotel touts who greet us at Tribhuvan Airport are as gentle as relief workers.

"No one will bother you here," our minivan driver assures us soothingly. "You are in Nepal now. This is not India."

No, it's not. It may be poorer than India, but the squalor here is less squalid, the chaos less chaotic. A backpackers' saying has it that India is an acronym for I'll Never Do India

Again, while Nepal stands for Never Ending Peace And Love. Missing hyphen aside, that seems about right.

We check into the Acme Guest House, in the touristy Thamel district. Our $12 room boasts satellite TV and a balcony that overlooks a garden. Andrea pronounces this tranquil setting the perfect place to finish reading *War and Peace*.

We take our first meal at the open-air Northfield Cafe, where Bach and Beethoven mix with the bougainvillea. We are surprised to find Mexican food on the menu and astonished when the burritos taste better than any we've had outside Mexico or the U.S.

Kathmandu fashions itself as the culinary capital of the subcontinent. If any cuisine is missing, it's probably on the way. We feast on pizza and listen to opera at the Italian restaurant Fire and Ice. At New Orleans, a jazz cafe, they serve a sumptuous jambalaya. And the outstanding Thai fare at Yin Yang is prepared by a chef from Thailand. Come breakfast, a German bakery is never more than a strudel's throw away.

This is also a literary city, with bookstores lining the streets. Competition keeps prices as low as $1.50 per paperback, and dealers will buy back books for 50% of what you paid. Everything from Austen to Zola is on the shelves. The selection at the two-story Pilgrims Book House is so marvelous and eclectic that it reminds me of browsing City Lights Bookstore, the San Francisco landmark.

If our eyes tire of reading, there are always the video bars, where pirated movies screen day and night. In the week after the Academy Awards, sidewalk chalkboards note show times for such Oscar-winning films as *American Beauty*, *The Cider House Rules* and *Boys Don't Cry*.

The comforts of Kathmandu are enhanced by Nepalis themselves. Like the Fijians we encountered early in our journey, they are quick with a smile. Their positive vibe is expressed in the greeting *"Namaste,"* which translates roughly as, "I salute the god within you."

Once we have decompressed, we hire a rickshaw to carry us to the sights. We visit Swayambhunath, also known as the Monkey Temple, where holy monkeys scamper over a hilltop Buddhist shrine; the palaces of Durbar Square; and Kasthamandap, a 16th century pagoda believed to be one of the oldest wooden buildings in the world.

It is a pleasure to tour temples and palaces without wannabe guides dogging your every step. Even the Tiger Balm hawkers are more likely to give you directions than a hard time. The stress-free atmosphere is reflected on the happy faces of the tourists, unlike in India, where we saw the strain of the streets reduce many Westerners to screams.

I catch myself whistling. I never whistle. Our journey suddenly feels lighter.

There is a downside to this giddy mood. The amenities that keep us here are ultimately harmful. A place that caters to tourists with foreign food, films and music leaves less room for its own culture. Also, I wonder if we have gone soft. Maybe we are not the intrepid travelers I imagined us to be. Perhaps we are ready for the cruise ship circuit, after all.

But these are concerns for another day. Today I see a Baskin-Robbins, and I feel like an ice cream.

Getting Connected
With the Itinerant Cafe Society

KATHMANDU, Nepal — We surfed in Fiji, New Zealand and India. We thought it would be tricky surfing in Nepal, but even here we found easy access to the Internet.

Circling the globe these days also involves navigating the World Wide Web. Cyber cafes along the tourist trail are now as common as hotels and souvenir stands. Aside from altering the look of the landscape, they are changing the way people travel.

Every long-term traveler we've met on this trip admits to breaking up the journey with at least the occasional session online. The typical traveler, Andrea and me included, ducks into an Internet shop once or twice a week. Most Net time is spent writing and reading e-mail, using one of the free e-mail providers such as Hotmail or Yahoo.

Besides e-mail, we have surfed the Net while abroad to make hotel reservations, research travel medicine questions and monitor activity on our credit card and bank accounts. Andrea has browsed the Web to buy birthday gifts, and I file this weekly column electronically, communicating with my editor via e-mail.

The world got wired in a hurry. When I last traveled at length five years ago, I did not see a single cyber cafe. Vagabonds sipped coffee in real cafes then, jotting stacks of postcards they dropped into dubious national mail systems, uncertain when and whether they would reach the intended recipients.

Today such folks are likely to be hunched over a keyboard in some side-street stall, firing their wish-you-were-heres around the planet instantaneously with a mouse click. I still see postcard vendors, but they look mighty bored.

Connection costs and speeds vary by country. Swift access to the Internet in New Zealand runs about $5 an hour. Some Japanese tourists in Christchurch thought this affordable enough to play video games online. It was not uncommon to see storefronts with 30 computers—and a body parked at each one. Modems for hire were everywhere we turned. We even spotted a coin-operated computer in a Subway sandwich shop in the town of Nelson.

Time online can be had for as little as 75 cents an hour in India, but the overburdened phone system means frequent crashes. The Indians make up for the poor quality with quantity. It seems everybody's brother is an Internet entrepreneur, even if his cyber cafe amounts to a PC and modem wedged into the corner of a sundries shop.

In Udaipur, a storekeeper gave me his seat behind the counter so I could log onto a computer that sat beneath shelves of cigarettes, film and toilet paper. In Jaisalmer, I wrote a column on a PC in somebody's living room while the boy of the house watched cricket on TV and Andrea entertained his baby sister on the couch.

At another Indian house turned cyber cafe, the family computer was only partially tucked under an exterior concrete stairway to the roof, mere inches from the street. Dirt from whoever was sweeping the roof rained down on the keyboard and my head, while sacred cows nudged my arm as they sauntered by.

The cyber surprise of the journey is Nepal. This tiny mountain kingdom lacks a freeway yet offers abundant onramps to the information superhighway. Signs for Internet shops dominate streets in the tourist section of the capital. The hardware and connections rival those found in cyber cafes in the States. Competition is so fierce that online rates have plummeted in the last two years, from $16 an hour to less than $1 an hour.

The advent of e-mail means that the world traveler is no longer disconnected from home. Nervous relatives can send reminders to be careful, co-workers can pass along office gossip and friends can provide laughs. We have met fellow wanderers who bemoan this electronic tether, but they still line up to log on.

Andrea and I send a monthly electronic update on our travels to about 60 relatives and friends, and many of them e-mail us back. Without the Internet, it would have been months before we heard that my sister, Debbie, had been accepted to medical school. Bill, our tenant, would be unable to convey the happy state of our pets. (Maya, our dog, has been sprayed by a skunk only once this year, a sharp decline from the same period a year ago.)

It was by e-mail that Robert, a Santa Barbara friend, warned us of a gem dealer in Agra, India, a certain Mr. Khan—"a crook, albeit a charming one." And when we sent a message to our friend Ron of Cincinnati, lamenting the alarming travel conditions in India, he slayed us with his brief reply: "When do you dial 911?"

It's funny how technology that was not widely available to travelers a few years ago now seems indispensable. At several points on this trip, I've logged on to retrieve information I easily did without on previous journeys. So far, I've gone online to scan headlines, check frequent-flier mileage, get sports scores and find match results at my local golf club. Entertaining, yes, but hardly essential.

My electronic trivial pursuits reached a nadir two months ago in New Zealand, where a familiar song got stuck in my head during a hike. Prompted by the sublime scenery I passed, the lyrics "It's all too beautiful" kept echoing in my mind. I did not know the name of the song or the band that recorded it, nor did any of the other people I pestered along the trail with my humming.

In another era, the repetitious refrain might still be bouncing around my noggin. But this is the year 2000. I went online, plugged the lyrics into the Metacrawler search engine and quickly learned that the tune tormenting me was "Itchycoo Park" by the 1960s group Small Faces. The answer came as a relief, and I'm happy to know that if another song gets lodged in my brain in Vietnam, Turkey or anyplace else down the road, a cyber cafe awaits me.

Savoring Some High Points
And Peak Experiences
In the Annapurna Range

POKHARA, Nepal — When I asked Nepali trekking guide Padam Magar the name of a distant, towering mountain—the tallest I had ever seen—he stifled a smile. "It has no name," he said. "It is not a mountain. It's just a ridge."

We soon rounded a bend in the trail that afforded a wider view. I froze in my tracks when the wall of white that had captivated me moments earlier was suddenly dwarfed by Dhaulagiri, the sixth-highest peak in the world. A plume of snow sailed from its 26,810-foot summit, and the only reason my jaw did not hit the ground was that I had to tilt my head back to take in the spectacle. "*That's* a mountain," Magar said.

In more ways than one, Andrea and I reached the high point of our journey thus far during a 13-day hike in the Himalayas. The stunning sights, hospitable people and remarkable food and lodging so far exceeded our expectations that we spent most of the trek wearing big, goofy grins. Long before we kicked off our hiking boots, we had vowed to return to these magical mountains.

We started in Pokhara, Nepal's second most popular tourist city, where we boarded a 25-minute flight north to the alpine village of Jomsom. The ascent was so steep, the 16-seat twin propeller plane never leveled off until it had landed on the dirt airstrip, its wings nearly clipping the mountain walls on approach.

After a day's hike farther north to Kagbeni, we turned around and gradually made our way back to Pokhara. We stuck mainly to the western leg of the Annapurna Circuit, a trail that follows a centuries-old Tibetan trade route along the Kali Gandaki River in the Annapurna mountain range. During the last several days, we walked east on a smaller trail that took us closer to the impressive Annapurna peaks.

We are not what you'd call outdoor types. Andrea has been backpacking all of two times, while most of my woods experience has been limited to hunting down errant golf balls. But we were ready for the Annapurna Circuit, also known as the Apple Pie Trek. Aside from the availability of the American dessert at nearly every inn along the way—usually cooked over an open fire—it is a relatively easy hike, attracting trekkers ages 8 to 80.

Still, we weren't taking any chances. Our path was smoothed by Kumar Magar (no relation to Padam), a porter we hired for $10 a day through a trekking agency in Kathmandu. He lashed our two rucksacks together and carried them on his back, leaving us to heft only our daypacks.

Kumar, 24, is part of an old Nepali tradition. As there are few roads in the Himalayas, most everything is transported on the backs of humans or donkeys. Our packs totaled 35 pounds, but it is not uncommon for a porter to carry four times that weight, the load braced by a strap across his forehead. Most wear flip-flops (Kumar had sneakers), but some walk barefoot. The cargo we saw men (and sometimes women) laboring under included sacks of rice, cases of beer, wood beams, 12-foot lengths of pipe and entire bed sets. Every time I sat on a Western-style toilet, I gave silent thanks to the poor porter who had schlepped it up the mountain.

We hiked three to seven hours a day, taking the occasional rest day in hamlets that offered the best views, rooms and enchiladas. The Himalayas handed us a new look each day—desert moonscapes, tumbling icefalls, terraced fields of buckwheat, forests of blooming rhododendrons. The one constant was the looming mountains. We hiked much of the time above 9,000 feet (I had no problems with the altitude, but Andrea had a mild headache the first night). That would place you at or near the top of most peaks in the Sierra Nevada. But in Nepal, it puts you only at the base of mountains that jut another three-plus vertical miles into the sky.

Hiking in this region of the Himalayas is never a solitary endeavor. You are always part of a human highway of porters, schoolchildren, other trekkers and pilgrims climbing to religious sites higher in the mountains. The trail, a marvel of engineering that features suspension bridges and miles of stone stairways, rarely stretches more than an hour between villages.

In Kagbeni, where colorful Buddhist prayer flags flap atop crumbling mud-brick houses, we wandered into the ancient Kag Chode Monastery. A young monk showed us a 700-year-old, 33-pound Tibetan prayer book penned in gold and silver. Outside, we ran our hands across rows of prayer wheels, canisters each containing a roll of paper inscribed repeatedly with the Tibetan Buddhist mantra *om mani padme hum* (hail to the jewel in the lotus). Each spin of the wheel, Buddhists believe, releases thousands of prayers into the heavens.

Midway through the trek, I realized I had no idea what day it was, and this gave me great pleasure. For the only extended period of my life, I became lost in the moment. Cut off from TV and radio, I tuned to natural rhythms: the jingle of a cowbell, the laugh of a child, the press of my boot against the earth.

Outside Kalopani, a group of us started single file across a rickety suspension bridge, careful not to step through the missing slats. An approaching line of donkeys, each bearing a heavy load, turned us back. The lead donkey wore a red plume on his head. The donkey driver wore a Walkman on his.

In Chomrong, a pleasant village clinging to a mountainside, I enjoyed the best shower of the trip. Not of the trek, but of our whole 3-month-old journey. The solar-heated shower at the Chomrong Guest House delivered a powerful stream of hot water, a rarity in these parts. What's more, the showerhead was high enough to accommodate my 6-foot-4 frame. Best of all, the concrete room had an open-air window that allowed me to gaze at Machhapuchhare, a perfectly proportioned peak that resembles a fish tail.

We had arrived early enough to secure Room 108. The coveted end room ($1.80 per night!) boasts windows on three sides, offering a panorama of the peaks Annapurna South,

Hiunchuli and Machhapuchhare. In the dining room we savored pizza alongside fellow trekkers from the U.S., Norway, Israel, Japan and Mexico while our feet were warmed by clay pots of hot coals beneath the communal table. Late in the day, we were visited by a triple rainbow. I went to sleep wondering if the trek could possibly get any better.

In the wee hours a bright light awakened me. A full moon shone on Annapurna South. The broad, snowy mountain now looked like a giant movie screen. I sat up in bed, not wanting the picture to end.

Tigers, Tuskers and Rhinos—Oh My! On a Subtropical Safari in Nepal

ROYAL CHITWAN NATIONAL PARK, Nepal — The great Indian one-horned rhinoceros looked unlike any I'd ever seen. This one wasn't in a cage.

The 2-ton beast lumbered from the forest, snapping fallen branches underfoot, halting in our path. My fears were not allayed by our position on the back of a pickup truck. Rhinos have poor vision and are liable to charge anything.

"Shoot it! Shoot it!" I implored Andrea. But as the rhino broke into a trot, Andrea discovered her camera was out of film, and the animal slipped into the trees.

"I didn't think we'd see one on the way to the hotel," Andrea said.

Neither did I. But that's Nepal, a small country with big surprises. After an unforgettable trek through the snowy Himalayas, the tiny kingdom continued to delight us during a three-day wildlife safari over subtropical plains. We had ventured south from Pokhara by bus, truck and riverboat to Royal Chitwan National Park, a 360-square-mile reserve on the Indian border. Besides rhinos, the park is home to leopards, sloth bears, several species of deer, two types of crocodiles and the elusive royal Bengal tiger.

We trashed our budget on this leg of the journey, checking into Temple Tiger, one of several upmarket lodges inside the park. The double rate is listed at $400 a night, but like everything in Nepal, this is negotiable. A bit of comparative shopping around Pokhara travel agencies reduced the price to $160, including meals, activities, park entrance fees and ground transportation.

We learned of the lodge from Harald and Lynn—he's a Norwegian graphic designer, she's an American nurse practitioner—a couple we met trekking. Our visit to the park happily coincided with theirs, and within a half-hour of our arrival, the four of us were atop two Asian elephants, riding into the jungle.

Harald was the only one among us who'd been on safari before, in Africa, and he found the encounter with wildlife in Nepal more natural. Andrea and I had no expectations, thrilled merely to bounce along on the back of an elephant. Our *pahit*, or elephant master, guided the animal with verbal commands and nudges behind the ears with his bare feet. The elephant knocked down small trees in its way and stuffed its mouth with grass yanked from the ground with its trunk. The slow rise-and-fall motion produced by the hulking mammal's gait evoked riding a bucking bronco across the bottom of a swimming pool.

My earlier concern over the missed photo opportunity was needless, as rhinos were everywhere we looked. Our *pahit* took glee in maneuvering the elephant close to the armored creatures, causing them to snort and stomp. As we gave chase, barking deer—animals the size of Labrador retrievers—scampered through the undergrowth.

Most visitors to Chitwan hope to glimpse a tiger, but few do. A worker told me he had not seen one the entire season. We spotted evidence of a tiger's presence—tracks in the sand along the Narayani River, a chewed-up deer leg—but no tiger.

Temple Tiger guests stay in individual elevated bungalows set well apart in the trees. Each unit has an attached bathroom, with solar-heated shower and marble floor inlaid with stone tiger paw prints. Woven wicker walls, spears and antlers add to the safari decor.

Our private balcony offered an idyllic place to enjoy the hoots and hollers of the park's 525 species of birds—had there been any time to use it. The neatly pressed staff kept us hopping dawn to dusk with river trips, nature walks and slide shows. A highlight was our encounter with an entertaining band of gray langur monkeys. The screeching primates leaped from tree to tree, grabbing branches that broke their falls like bungee cords.

We ate meals on bronze plates in an elegantly rustic, screened dining house, complete with sunken fireplace. Some of the food was familiar (onion quiche), some not (water buffalo), all of it delicious. After every few bites, a team of Nehru-jacketed waiters rushed in to scoop more food onto our platters.

The tea and coffee delivered to our deck at 5:30 the next morning served as a wake-up call for the sunrise safari. We were a full group, so Harald, Lynn, Andrea and I shared an elephant, each taking a corner of the howdah, the wooden-railed, padded riding platform. The jungle was bathed in an orange glow, dewy grass and spider webs glistening in the early light.

I marveled at how the mass of gray beneath us managed to glide through the bush in near silence, but after 90 minutes we had sighted nothing more than two rhinos. When our elephant turned for home, blazing a different trail from the others, I figured we were ending an uneventful, but pleasant, ride.

At last something new appeared. A large spotted deer now stood frozen in the tall grass to our left. It eyed us nervously as the elephant abruptly stopped.

"Tiger," the *pahit* whispered, making me think he did not know the English word for the animal we observed. Goose bumps sprang from my flesh when I realized he was looking elsewhere. And I felt my heart in my throat when I swiveled my head and took in the giant striped cat lurking about 100 feet in front of us.

"Oh, my God!" I blurted.

"Oh! Oh! Oh!" gasped Lynn, pounding on the *pahit's* shoulders.

The tiger was beautiful but scowling, perhaps miffed that we had come between it and breakfast. I did not blink, afraid it might approach or, worse, vanish. But like magic, the magnificent cat melted into the forest.

The *pahit* checked his watch and aimed the elephant toward the lodge. For some of us in the jungle, breakfast was waiting.

A Week of Sundays

SIEM REAP, Cambodia — The blues always come on a Sunday, in the afternoon, when the simplest things don't compute, and malaise plops beside me, drapes its heavy arm across my shoulders and says, "Mind if I stay for dinner?"

At home, I step out of Sunday's way and wait for Monday. But the Wander Year doesn't run on a regular calendar, and out here Sunday can strike any day of the week—and linger.

Sunday finds me on a Friday in Nepal, stalks me to Thailand and chases me into Cambodia, not letting go until Thursday.

"We gotta get it together, baby," I sing to Andrea all week long. But it's a big joke. I can't sing and Andrea has it together. Sunday doesn't mess with her.

My week of Sundays is ignited by sudden moves and fueled by fast food. Unless you journey by foot, rapid, disorienting travel is an unavoidable side effect of any trip around the world. Now toss in a few greasy gut grenades, and you're just begging to get slammed by a Sunday tsunami.

I sniff out the McDonald's near our hotel in central Bangkok, down the road from Burger King, close to Dunkin' Donuts, around the corner from the Dairy Queen, next door to KFC. Before you can say, "Super size it!" I'm on the Mother of All Fast Food Binges.

Fast food in Thailand is genuinely fast, adding a touch of the unreal to my sorry endeavor. The cashiers hop from foot to foot like kids who need to use the bathroom, practically climbing over the counter to take your order. The food arrives before your change.

A couple days go by and I try to break the cycle with a stop at Au Bon Pain, the relatively healthy bakery and deli chain. It's no use. I suffer Whopper withdrawal and my butt's back at Burger King by noon. The only thing to do now is grab more napkins and hold on tight.

Junk-food joints anchor a four-block swath of mega-malls in the heart of Bangkok that appear to have rebounded from the Asian financial crisis. Young, prosperous-looking Thais chat on cellphones as they race from the Athlete's Foot to the Nike store to the Body Shop. When they stop to rest, there's no room at Starbucks to sit and sip my venti iced latte.

A vast network of crisscrossing skywalks and escalators that keep people moving and shopping connects the gleaming high-rise malls.

"Visit Tomorrowland today," Andrea says.

We enter the sprawling Siam Discovery Center shopping complex. After Andrea buys a new pair of Ray-Bans and I cruise the video arcade, we duck into a multiscreen movie theater to catch *The Whole Nine Yards*. In the dark, reclining in my plush, high-backed seat, I'm thinking, "This could be America"—until the audience is suddenly on its feet, paying homage to His Majesty Bhumibol Adulyadej, king of Thailand, whose image flickers on the screen.

Bruce Willis, Coke, Levi's…Has our culture taken over the world, or has the world taken over our culture? I ponder this further over a Big Mac.

I hate fast food and malls. But four months of strange menus and stranger sights can send you scurrying for the familiar—even though the familiar is the stuff you usually detest.

Now that I'm shaking from a diet of sugar, fat and caffeine, I hurl myself at the logistics of onward travel. Our visas for Vietnam are not valid for another three days, so we plan a jaunt to Cambodia.

Andrea wants to fly, which means more hasty, sensibility-warping motion. I want to ride 20 hours in the back of a pickup over a bumpy dirt road. Andrea wins, and I sulk about it over a final hot fudge sundae at Dairy Queen.

I down my weekly dose of Lariam. The antimalarial boosts my frenzy. I wonder whether the disease is any worse than the prevention.

We land here in the provincial capital of Siem Reap. In the near future, this gateway to the Angkor region will transform into a major tourist hub; but in 2000, it remains a sleepy backwater, only now emerging from decades of bloody repression.

I'm struck by the jocularity of Cambodians, considering their recent genocidal past. Our guide, Phirum Proeun, starts with ancient history but quickly segues into more modern events. He says his father was a provincial army leader who was killed in 1975 by Pol Pot's Khmer Rouge. Proeun chops his neck with his hand to show how as he lets out a little chuckle.

We tour the famed temples of Angkor, including Angkor Wat, built by the Khmer civilization between the 9th and 13th centuries. The structures are awesome, ornate and eerie. I think of shopping malls.

A crack of lightning and a sudden downpour send us running for the shelter of a banyan-entwined temple, its walls pocked with bullet holes. Inside, several amputees, their limbs lost to landmines that still dot the surrounding area, rest on the cool stone floor.

An old woman with a shaved head pounds her fists on my chest, back and buttocks, and blows in my face.

"She is blessing you," Proeun says.

The rain subsides, and we climb a nearby temple, scaling a steep, metal ladder bolted in the wall. On top, my acrophobia kicks in, and I can't bring myself to climb back down the ladder. Instead, I hang by my fingertips from a massive stone block and drop to a landing 12 feet below. I repeat the procedure at several more blocks until I reach the ground.

"What are you doing?" Andrea keeps shouting at me. "Are you crazy?"

Well…

Proeun drives us back to town and drops us at a Thai restaurant. Now that I'm in Cambodia, I eat the food I never got around to eating in Thailand.

That night, at the Freedom Hotel, I read a sign posted on our closet door: "It is against hotel regulations to have firearms or explosives in your room without our approval."

Almost over, the week finally starts making sense.

A Visit to Vietnam
Brings an Attitude Adjustment

HO CHI MINH CITY, Vietnam — Like many Americans, I've always regarded Vietnam as a symbol more than a place.

I grew up during the Vietnam War watching Walter Cronkite report body counts on the nightly news. The grim specter of Vietnam took form in my mind through such films as *The Deer Hunter, Apocalypse Now* and *Platoon*. The image was fixed with my move in the 1980s to Washington, D.C., where I occasionally visited the Vietnam Veterans Memorial wall, that granite gash in the ground that evokes an open wound on the nation.

The word "Vietnam" conjures tragedy, shame and folly. So when our journey brings us to this Southeast Asian country, I expect to flip through the pages of a sad chapter from U.S. history. No surprise, reminders of the war are abundant and strong. The shocker is that I also find a pleasant and user-friendly tourist destination.

After brief visits to Thailand and Cambodia, Andrea and I fly to this city formerly known as Saigon, where my preconceptions are challenged the moment we land at Tan Son Nhat airport. Because Vietnam is a Communist nation, I brace for a tangle with bureaucracy. We instead breeze through the easiest immigration process of our trip.

Within 10 minutes, we've traded dollars for *dong* and are riding toward the city center in a new air-conditioned taxi. Outside our window zoom some of the city's 1.4 million motorcycles. Many are straddled by women wearing *ao dai*, the graceful traditional garb.

At the Hanh Hoa Hotel, in the tourist area of Pham Ngu Lao, a young staff that's all smiles and eager to please greets us. We can't pass through the lobby without at least one worker leaping to his feet to offer assistance. Every time we retrieve our room key, the receptionist escorts us to the elevator.

Our room is the cleanest we've had since New Zealand. The bathroom contains shower sandals and new toothbrushes. The mini-bar is stocked with Coke and Pringles. Satellite TV and ample lighting—rare amenities on this journey—are welcome additions. You're supposed to bargain for everything here, but when the first room rate tossed out is $15, I can't find the nerve to dicker.

Vietnam's leaders run a quasi-capitalist economy, allowing some citizens to own small businesses. The neighborhood around our hotel is thick with Internet shops, travel agencies and cheap cafes that give diners chilled washcloths before meals. We eat at the inevitably named Good Morning Vietnam Restaurant, where they serve up tasty pizza and pasta.

This city retains some vestiges of its French colonial past, such as broad, tree-lined boulevards. We glide by elegant buildings on hired cyclos, pedicabs with the passenger seat in front of the bike. In the fashionable Dong Khoi area, we pop into a bistro for croissants and espresso, and for a minute we're in Paris.

Still, Vietnam won't be confused with the West any time soon. This remains one of the poorest countries in the world. Street hawkers are polite but persistent, exuding an air of desperation. The sidewalks teem with beggars, many of them crippled by land mines left over from the war. We are told not to give money to female panhandlers with babies, many of whom rent the infants from poor families to appear more needy and feed them sleeping pills to keep them quiet.

But the eye is quickly drawn to prettier sights.

On a drive south to the Mekong Delta, we are dazzled by the sublime landscape, counting no fewer than six shades of green. Peasants tend rice paddies by hand, fending off the sun with conical straw hats.

At the Mekong River, we board a boat that cruises by floating markets, where weathered wooden vessels sit half-submerged under loads of produce, their bows emblazoned with painted red dragon eyes to scare whatever evil lurks in the water.

As our boat motors down one of the countless canals, children race along the bank, waving and shouting, "Hello! Hello!" We pull ashore to test our balance on a few of the region's 300,000 single-log footbridges, our awkward efforts drawing giggles from the kids. I spot two boys in a ramshackle stilted house playing with a pink plastic sword. I show them how to fake a deep stab by sliding the sword between my arm and body. When I leave, the boys are writhing on the plank floor in mock death throes.

Back in Ho Chi Minh City, we enter the most popular tourist attraction dedicated to what is known here as the American War. The War Remnants Museum is heavy on propaganda, presenting only one side of the conflict. Even so, some of the pictures and exhibits are so ghastly that I wince and look away. Also jarring is the sight of captured American tanks and aircraft on display in a foreign land. Souvenir stands sell Zippo lighters and dog tags that allegedly once belonged to U.S. soldiers.

We continue our tour of the war with a guided visit to the Cu Chi tunnels, 35 miles northwest of the city. It was from a 125-mile-long network of tunnels in this district that Viet Cong guerrillas planned and launched attacks on the enemy, living underground for weeks on end. American measures to disable the tunnels—bombs, bulldozers, defoliants, ground troops, even dogs—failed. Crawling on my hands and knees, I can practically read the history of our defeat in Vietnam on the dirt walls of these ingenious tunnels.

On the ride back into town, our guide speaks of the unified Vietnam. Whether from north or south, Vietnamese are first brothers and sisters, he says. People have forgiven the past and now focus on the future. The guide was a soldier in the defeated South Vietnamese army, so I don't know whether his sentiments are genuine or the product of his time in a reeducation camp.

Either way, he has a point. The war ended 25 years ago. I doubt Vietnam will cease being a dark symbol to me, but after a few days here, it already occupies a brighter corner of my mind.

A Hamlet Tailor-Made for Repose

HOI AN, Vietnam — The word of mouth on Hoi An had become a gathering chorus.

We first heard of this town near Vietnam's central coast way back in Fiji, during the early days of our journey. An Australian woman we met at a beach resort had been here three times. Raves for Hoi An followed us wherever we went, from New Zealand to Cambodia. "You've got to go there," some traveler always seemed to be gushing. "You'll love it."

Andrea and I were soon certain of a visit here. The only question was whether Hoi An would live up to the hype. Much to our delight, it exceeded it.

Little Hoi An is a part of Vietnam but a world apart. Sitting on the Thu Bon River three miles from the South China Sea and about midway between Hanoi and Ho Chi Minh City, it retains an Old World charm from its days as a thriving port of call for Dutch, Portuguese, Japanese and Chinese trading ships. Unblemished by the Vietnam War, the pretty hamlet belongs more to the 17th century than to the 21st.

We knew we had arrived somewhere special when our taxi south from the Da Nang airport parked several blocks from our hotel. The historical heart of town is closed to vehicles, helping us imagine we had been transported back in time. We carried our bags down narrow streets, past faded yellow buildings with green shutters. The roofs are topped with clay tiles, and silk brocade Chinese lanterns hang from the eaves. Day or night, the town fairly glows.

At the Vinh Hung Hotel, an old building that was once a Chinese trading house, we were shown to the Antiques Room, the inn's most elegant quarters. The $30-a-night room boasts a four-poster bed with canopy and lace curtains. Other antiques, including an inlaid mother-of-pearl desk, sit against walls of rich ebony wood. The one concession to modernity, a remote-controlled air conditioner, was welcome relief from the stifling heat.

There is little to do in Hoi An but linger and soak up the atmosphere. This is a stylish place, where young women wearing smart crocheted hats pedal bikes through the streets. Most of the sights—ethnic Chinese assembly halls, old private homes, a restored covered bridge originally built by the Japanese community in 1593—are accessible by foot, allowing visitors to browse art galleries along the way.

Hoi An's spot on Vietnam's culinary map is claimed by *cao lau*, a simple but sumptuous mix of thick noodles, bean sprouts, croutons, greens and pork slices, served in a soup bowl. Another local dish that pleased our taste buds and eyes was "white rose," a plate of shrimp individually wrapped in wide noodles and folded into flower shapes.

All of the restaurants we tried were good, but the Tam Tam Cafe & Bar was exceptional. We dined on the balcony of the restored tea warehouse, feasting on duck and homemade noodles while listening to recorded jazz. For dessert, I scarfed down the best profiteroles I've had outside France.

After three days of grazing and lazing, we decided to do something constructive. Or, I should say, we hired some people to do something constructive. Hoi An is known for its many fabric stores, where expert tailors can turn out a suit of clothes for less than the cost of alterations in the States.

Andrea and I occupy opposite positions on the fashion front. She has a humongous wardrobe and needs little excuse to expand it. All my clothes fit in a laundry bag, yet I'm always keen to pare down. In their respective ways, two Hoi An tailors accommodated both of us.

Andrea settled on the My My Cloth Shop, lauded by previous customers in a letter posted at our hotel. She was measured for a skirt, pantsuit and three blouses—all silk. The clothes were ready overnight, fit perfectly and totaled $53.

I assumed all Hoi An tailors are equally skilled and followed an adorable 16-year-old tout to her mother's shop in the market. Seated in a toy chair at a toy table and offered a toy cup of tea, I flipped through a J. Crew catalog, stopping at a page depicting a dashing man in an off-white summer suit. Sure, I figured, why not? A pair of women traded giggles as they ran a measuring tape over every inch of my body and jotted down various numbers. The only truly ridiculous figure was the price—$30.

When I returned the next day for my $30 suit, it looked like, well, a $30 suit. The thread did not match the fabric, the material puckered and the jacket gave me the range of motion of a mummy. I donated it to whomever might find it in our hotel room.

Before leaving town, I stopped by Andrea's tailor. I wanted something to remind me of this place. I was measured for an outfit that, like Hoi An, is classy yet relaxed—silk pajamas.

Fear of Flying, Floating and Fatality

HANOI — Whoever said getting there is half the fun never shared a berth on a Vietnamese train with two uninvited bunkmates. Or raced down a putrid canal on a Thai water taxi. Or crashed into a ditch on an Indian auto-rickshaw.

When Andrea and I set out around the globe, we knew we'd spend a lot of time getting from point A to point B, and beyond. What we didn't foresee was the myriad modes of transportation we would use, most offering some level of discomfort, distress and danger.

Traveling in the developing world is like visiting a rundown amusement park. The rides are cheap, but you half expect the roller coaster to fly off the rails and slam into the cotton candy stand.

Several times a day here in Hanoi, we climb into a contraption called a cyclo, a cousin of the rickshaw. The driver pedals from behind the passengers, giving you the sensation of riding in a runaway wheelchair. The key is to keep your arms and legs out of the way of the gazillion scooters and other cyclos hurtling at you from every direction.

Besides the common plane, train, automobile, bus and rickshaw, we've seen the world by foot, ice shoes, elephant, minibus, bike, aerial tramway, ferry, catamaran, canoe, raft, motorboat, rowboat, jet boat, longboat and slow boat. Some of these means of transport evoke medieval instruments of torture, squeezing you into a space that forces you to ride with your knees up by your ears.

Our strangest trip in Vietnam was an overnight train from Hue to Hanoi. We paid $55 each for a "soft sleeper," Communist Vietnam's politically correct term for a first-class berth. But the foreigner's fare—16 times more than what Vietnamese pay for a hard sleeper—does not buy privacy.

Around dawn I was awakened by the cackles of train workers who decided to take a break in our sleeping compartment. I peered down from my top bunk and found two women sitting on Andrea's bed, eating hard-boiled eggs, throwing the shells on the floor. They inspected a few of Andrea's things, taking special interest in a photo of our dog, Maya. Andrea, who is not a morning person, rolled her eyes and curled up in a ball.

Our transportation experiences in Vietnam have been mostly positive. The minivans, in particular, are efficient, convenient and clean. But like anywhere else in the world, sometimes even the shortest rides can get complex. One Hanoi cabbie padded the fare by driving us in the wrong direction. After I showed him I knew the right way by pointing at a map, he tried one more trick. The meter read 29,000 *dong*, when we reached our hotel. But with a touch of a button, the fare jumped to 51,000 *dong*. The driver denied changing the meter and insisted I pay the latest price.

He agreed to accept the lower of the two dubious fares only after I threatened to complain to authorities.

The cheapest trip of our journey to date was a 15-cent ride on a water taxi down the Khlong Saen Saep, a canal through Bangkok, Thailand. The low fare did not include such frills as stops. You literally jump on and off the overcrowded motorboat as it briefly slows down. The foul canal—it looks as though it could burn—puts the needed spring in your step to clear the water.

The scariest transportation moment of the journey so far came in Varanasi, India, where we took our last ride in an auto-rickshaw, a sort of mini-cab on three wheels. We should have seen we were at risk when the driver stopped to add brake fluid. The brakes failed a mile later when the driver tried to slow for an onrushing car borrowing our lane. He steered the speeding rickshaw to the shoulder, where we closed in on the backs of three female pedestrians, two of them carrying babies. At the last instant, we plowed into a pile of dirt, and the rickshaw stopped in a freshly dug ditch.

The driver rushed from the rickshaw and paid another rickshaw driver 20 *rupees* to take us the rest of the way. I took this as an apology and checked my urge to yell at him. But after we got into the second rickshaw, he reached in and demanded the 150 *rupees* we had agreed to pay him before the wreck, a debt I assumed had been canceled by his flagrant negligence. Too stunned to protest, and a little impressed by his chutzpah, I handed him the money.

"Buy some brakes," Andrea said.

Before we left the U.S., I stumbled across airsafe.com, a Web site that lists fatality rates for airlines around the world. We planned to avoid carriers with poor or unreported safety records. But after a few too many long, sweaty bus rides, we now hop on anything that flies, including Sahara Airlines (India), Gorkha Airlines (Nepal) and Royal Air Cambodge (Cambodia), none of which are tracked by airsafe.com.

I reflected on our drop in standards during a recent flight from Siem Reap to Ho Chi Minh City on Vietnam Airlines, another carrier that keeps a tight grip on safety figures. When I visited the bathroom, the door pulled off its hinges.

Rather than panic, I took it as a good sign. It meant money was invested in some other part of the plane. I hoped it was the landing gear.

In China,
Away From the Bothersome
Tourist Hype

NANNING, China — For one blissful day I'm not a tourist. I blend into the crowd; I feel invisible. I'm just another 6-foot-4-inch blue-eyed dude in China.

There are 2 million people in this city, and not one of them is pushing postcards, trinkets or T-shirts on me. I'm irrelevant to the economy of this booming commercial hub. I've wandered off the tourist track back into the real world. Nanning is the Fresno of China, and it's my new favorite place.

Andrea and I are en route from Hanoi, to Guilin, a popular destination in the southern Chinese province of Guangxi. There are no direct flights. We must fly to Nanning, about 350 miles west of Hong Kong, spend the night, then catch a 45-minute flight to Guilin in the morning.

I know we've left Lonely Planetland behind when we clear customs and aren't mobbed by the usual throng of touts. The shiny, modern terminal is eerily quiet. The only sound I hear is the click of nails as a Pekingese scampers across the marble floor, a woman giving silent chase.

The young teller at the airport bank says I can't change money there. At least I think that's what he's saying. China is the first country on this trip where we've run into a language barrier. I walk away, wondering how we'll get into town without any Chinese *yuan*.

I return to ask the teller where I can change money. He tries to say something in English, but I again leave confused. The man seems really friendly, as though he'd help if he could, so I go back and press a $100 bill to the window. He either pities me or now understands what I'm after, taking the bill and sliding me the equivalent in *yuan*. I thank him profusely. He smiles and says, "Have enjoyable time China."

We spot a row of business-type hotel information booths. None of the representatives speaks English. We flip through a few brochures. The hotels look nice, but the rates are beyond our budget. The agent from the Ming Yuan Hotel writes "-30%" on the tariff sheet and smiles. A three-star hotel for $25 a night. We smile back.

She leads us to a bus filled with Asian men talking on cellphones. She gets in behind us and sits across the aisle. I don't know whether she's heading into town anyway or making a special trip for our benefit. We trade more smiles.

When we stop at a traffic light, I see a girl straddling a bike on the grass median. Her eyes grow big, and she starts laughing her head off. I turn to see what's so funny, then realize she's laughing at Andrea and me. It occurs to me what oddities we are here. When the light turns green, she's doubled over her bike in hysterics.

The Ming Yuan is even better than advertised. The hotel is set in wooded grounds dotted with gardens and ponds and features a large swimming pool, tennis courts and bowling alley. Best of all, the karaoke bar is nowhere near our room. The woman who brings us here disappears before I can say *"xiexie"* ("thank you," pronounced quickly as "she-yeah she-yeah"), the only Mandarin I know.

Andrea has a touch of something, so she rests in our clean, comfortable room while I explore the city. I hit the street in my defensive mode—eyes fixed straight ahead, purposeful stride. I'm steeled for the onslaught I've come to expect: the rickshaw drivers who follow you for blocks, ringing their bells; the peddlers who shove woodcarvings in your face; the vendors who, under the pretext of making conversation, start their pitches with the same three words, "Where you from?"

I get none of that. No one calls to me, chases me, grabs me. In the most populous country on the planet, I finally find some space. Today I'm not a giant wallet walking down the street. I'm something else, something close to human.

Relaxed, guard dropped, I can focus again and see what a lovely city this is. Large, leafy trees form a canopy over broad boulevards. Bicyclists pedal in their own lane. The wide sidewalks are lined with benches. The city center is busy yet peaceful. In Nanning, unlike other Asian cities we've visited, motorists don't drive with one hand on the horn.

I step under an archway and enter People's Park. A forested hillside tumbles down to a pretty lake, where people row boats in the foreground of a gleaming skyline. Couples stroll hand in hand down shady paths. A maintenance truck rumbles by. The worker standing in back bashfully returns my wave.

I walk for hours, content to watch others go about their daily lives. I pass dress shops, electronics stores, beauty parlors, banks, office buildings. Nothing I see is aimed at the tourist, and that's just dandy.

Although nobody approaches or speaks to me, I eventually notice the stares. Some people stop in their tracks to look me up and down. A man eating in a cafeteria points me out to the little boy bouncing on his knee. I peer at a window display of electronic pagers and see teenage girls on the other side giggling at me.

At last someone stops me to talk.

"Hello," the man says.

"Hello," I say.

"Bye-bye," he says.

"Bye-bye," I say.

We let our big grins say the rest.

In the morning, a bellman carries our backpacks to the taxi. The driver asks us something in Chinese. "Airport," I tell her. She doesn't understand. I hold my arms out like wings, pretending to be an airplane. She looks at me as though I'm nuts. Maybe I am. Why would I leave this place?

In Search of a Guide
Never to be Met

YANGSHUO, China — We planned to skip China, but Jenny Xu changed our minds.

We learned of the 26-year-old tour guide through Lynn and Harald, the couple we traveled with in Nepal and Thailand.

"You've got to ask for her," Lynn had enthused. "She's just adorable."

When they came here last winter, Jenny took them on a bike ride to her village, cooked them lunch in her home and charmed them with her humor. Lynn and Harald's day with Jenny was one of the high points of their journey.

That made Andrea and me keen to visit China. Armed with the name Jenny Xu (pronounced shoo), we no longer thought the country so overwhelming and impersonal. We could not see it all, but we could venture here and let Jenny show us her corner of the world.

Yangshuo, about 300 miles northwest of Hong Kong, is one of those rare places that defies comparisons. This town on the Li River is surrounded for miles by towering limestone pinnacles blanketed in green. The lush landscape looked so otherworldly and prehistoric that I could picture dinosaurs craning their necks around the spiked rock formations.

A crowd of freelance tour guides greeted us at the bus station.

We already have a guide, we told them.

Who? several young women asked, following us down the street.

Jenny Xu, we said.

Our answer prompted a flurry of cryptic comments in broken English:

"Jenny not here."

"Jenny gone."

"Big water take Jenny Xu."

When we reached the Hotel Explorer, the receptionist confirmed what we had begun to fear: Jenny was dead.

Four days earlier, heavy rains had turned a small, gentle tributary of the Li into a giant, angry torrent. When the storm let up, Jenny was the only one to lead tourists on a bike ride through the country. Other guides told her to stay in town, that the dirt road along the stream would be flooded. No one said why she insisted on going, but the fact that her unemployed husband lost money gambling and the couple had a 4-year-old daughter to feed may have had something to do with it.

Jenny and her two clients pedaled past rice paddies that stretch out across the earth amid the scenic soaring spires. When they reached a point where water flowed over the road, Jenny said she would go first. She started to push her bike across the stream and was swept away by the current. A British tourist jumped in after her and nearly drowned before the current spit him out within reach of the bank.

Jenny's body was not found.

We wandered the flagstone streets of Yangshuo, trying to learn more from locals about the young woman who had brought us here. It seemed everybody knew and liked her. There was only one Jenny. (Like many here, she had adopted a Western name to make it easy for tourists.) Wherever she went, people waved and called to her. She liked to laugh and crack jokes. Most of all, they recalled that she adored her little girl, how Jenny was always riding the child around on her bike.

"We only spent a day with her, but the time was so special I feel like I have lost a good friend," Lynn e-mailed me after I told her of Jenny's death. "The world works in such cruel ways. She just loved to talk about her daughter, and now I wonder who will take her to school and watch her grow up."

Lynn added: "This is such a loss for Yangshuo. Jenny really brought a lot of happiness to people."

In the lobby of our hotel, we met Li Li Mo, one of the guides who tried to talk Jenny out of working that last day. Li Li and Jenny were friends, both raised in the nearby village of Moon Hill. For 60 *yuan* (about $7.25), Li Li spent half a day taking us to all the places we had planned to see with Jenny.

We rode bikes along dirt lanes that meander through green fields beneath the unearthly peaks. The scenery I had found so stunning on the bus ride into town now made me sad.

After a few miles, Li Li stopped pedaling.

"There's Jenny," she said.

I did not understand her until I noticed we had stopped by a stream. The wild water that had claimed Jenny was now still. A farmer tended the edge of an adjacent rice paddy, turning the soil with a hoe.

We had nearly pedaled off before I saw the shrine. A purple blouse—its corners tied to the tops of four reeds—fluttered in the wind. Incense sticks burned in the mud. Half-buried in the earth, a pair of women's sneakers, their soles facing up.

Before we came to this country, I read that a famine in the late 1950s and early 1960s killed 30 million Chinese. The number is so immense that it is beyond my comprehension. It seems unreal. I don't know what to call it. But one name, one life, one makeshift memorial on a riverbank—I know the word for that: tragic.

Goodbye, Jenny Xu. Sorry we never met.

Effortlessly Enjoying Local Color Amid the Canals and Cobblestones Of Lijiang

LIJIANG, China — We didn't do much last week. Didn't need to. We were in Lijiang.

This is an effortless travel destination. You needn't seek out activities, performances and events to enjoy the place. Its character and culture are on display every day in the streets, a living museum. All you need do is show up.

The old town of Lijiang, the nucleus of a modern city of the same name, looks much as it did when it was settled 800 years ago, during the transition between the Song and Yuan dynasties. It is the base for China's colorful Naxi (pronounced nah-shee) minority, descendants of Tibetan nomads, who constitute most of the old town's 40,000 residents. Their home is a marvelous maze of cobblestone streets, narrow canals and weathered wooden buildings.

Lijiang lies in a green valley 7,900 feet above sea level, in the upper reaches of Yunnan province, near the Tibetan border. The region enjoys spring-like conditions most of the year. Locals claim that their streets never get dusty in summer, or muddy in winter.

This was our last stop on a three-week tour of southwest China, which also included visits to Kunming, the provincial capital, and Dali, home of the Bai minority. Of all the countries Andrea and I have passed through on this journey, China has held the most surprises. Its stunning scenery, outstanding cuisine and warm, helpful people far exceeded our expectations.

Our taxi from the Lijiang bus station stopped where pavement gives way to cobblestone. The only wheels allowed in the old town must belong to bicycles or carts.

The twisting streets teemed with women dressed in traditional Naxi outfits of blue blouses and pants, worn under vibrant aprons. Old men in blue caps puffed on pipes. Cats dozed in doorways.

The red wooden dwellings are so uniform—each topped with gray ornamental tiles and a crown line with upturned ends—it's hard to tell those built centuries ago from those built last year. Typically, three generations live in a complex of one main house and two side houses, or in one large structure set around a courtyard.

The architecture owes a lot to nearby cultures. The Naxi borrowed tile and brick making from the Han, China's dominant ethnic group; woodcarving designs from the Bai; and wall painting styles from the Tibetans.

The hybrid structures have served the Naxi well. On Feb. 3, 1996, the area was hit by a 7.0-magnitude earthquake. It killed 309 people and devastated the new part of the city, but most of old town Lijiang was still standing.

Lijiang boasts an ingenious and intricate water system. Glacial runoff from Jade Dragon Snow Mountain, an 18,000-foot peak 20 miles north, reaches Lijiang via the Yu-He River. As the river approaches the city, it splits into three streams, which are diverted into 10 canals that wend through the old town.

The canals, lined by willow trees and potted marigolds, flow by every home, providing residents with water and a place to do laundry, wash dishes and rinse vegetables. Houses, shops and restaurants are accessed by tiny stone or wood bridges, under which floats the occasional youth on a tire tube.

Such a tranquil and harmonious setting naturally draws visitors. Lijiang is especially popular with domestic tourists, although new cafes specializing in banana pancakes and Bob Marley tunes point to an influx of Westerners. Tourism and outside influences are changing the social fabric. Some Naxi, seduced by high rents offered by Han entrepreneurs, have leased their homes and moved out.

Still, Lijiang is one of the more authentic spots we've visited. This is a place where it's actually fun to get lost. One night an aimless stroll led us to the patio of Mama Fu's Restaurant. The manager sat with us, patiently making recommendations in broken English.

We settled on the sweet-and-sour fish. The chef soon emerged from the kitchen, waded into the canal and wrangled a live fish from a cage submerged in the clear, rushing water. Moments later, the cooked fish was presented to us on a platter. I don't know if it was the best I ever tasted, but it had to be the freshest.

Considering its age, Lijiang seems a youthful town. Children are given the run of the streets, where they kick soccer balls and play badminton. On our last night, a girl of about 3 handed Andrea a balloon, instructing her to hold it by the string. The little girl laughed with glee as she repeatedly batted the balloon with her hand. All Andrea had to do was stand there like a tetherball pole.

As I said, Lijiang demands little of the visitor.

Prodded and Pummeled Into Paradise At a Thai Spa

KO SAMUI, Thailand — I studied the menu of massage packages at the Tamarind Springs spa: "Traditional Thai," "Sheer Indulgence," "Divine Decadence." They looked good, but none was just what I craved.

I decided to order off the menu.

The receptionist took notes as I described my ultimate spa fantasy. I'd start with an herbal steam sauna, follow that with a two-hour traditional Thai full-body massage, continue with a half-hour facial and polish the day off with a half-hour wild mint foot massage.

The only problem was that my "package" didn't have a cute little name.

"What do you call this?" I asked.

"Extreme," the receptionist said.

A tad, perhaps. But if you're going to be a bear, might as well be a grizzly.

The setting for my massage marathon was Ko Samui, an island in the Gulf of Thailand, about 275 miles south of Bangkok. After three weeks in China, Andrea and I had returned to Thailand, the crossroads of Southeast Asia.

Thai massage, a blend of acupressure and manipulation, is a cottage industry here. Throw a coconut and you're bound to hit a masseuse. They work on the beach, in studios and in resorts like Tamarind Springs.

My spa visit was more or less a medical emergency. My body had been ravaged by the rigors of globe-trotting. The day before, I had dragged a beach chair into the sea and sat in the warm, clear water. I couldn't survive another day of such strenuous activity without serious rejuvenation.

I'm not really a spa guy. My few previous massages have induced, rather than reduced, stress; I lay there the whole time fretting about the cost.

But massage in Thailand is cheaper than a meal in a budget restaurant. The freelancers on the beach, many of whom trained under massage masters in Buddhist temples, charge about $5 per hour. Even the obscene swath I planned to cut through Tamarind Springs would set me back less than $50. At that price, I could afford to be extreme—and relaxed.

Unlike most resorts on this cramped, touristy island, Tamarind Springs sits far from the beach. The airy, thatched structures dot the side of a mountain thick with coconut palms. Joining me there was Andrea, who countered my gluttony with a mere 90-minute session.

I traded my clothes for a plaid sarong and climbed the path to the herbal steam sauna, built between two giant boulders, the rocks serving as walls. Shafts of sunlight pierced the steam through translucent glass tiles in the ceiling. Under a rocky overhang outside the door is a cold plunge pool. Padding from sauna to pool to refrigerator stocked with mineral water and iced ginger tea, I nearly melted into the mountainside.

After showering and changing into a fresh sarong, I met Toey, my masseuse. She was a slight woman, yet she had forearms like howitzers. I would be under their power for the next three hours.

Toey led me up the hill to a thatched platform where other masseuses in blue surgeon's pants and floral blouses labored over tourists stretched out on elevated mats. Lying on my back, I closed my eyes and listened to the whir of overhead fans, the strains of New Age music and the flutter of palm fronds—punctuated by frequent sighs of bliss from my neighbors.

Toey had worked 30 minutes on my right leg when it dawned on me just how long three hours is. My massage would last longer than a movie, longer than a baseball game, even longer than some of history's pivotal battles. Maybe I had crossed the line between indulgence and overindulgence. I felt a twinge of guilt, which vanished when Toey began kneading my left calf.

Traditional Thai massage involves 68 positions, few of which I'd have thought I could be folded into. Toey used her hands, elbows, knees, legs and feet to pull, twist, stretch, jab, stomp, poke, pound and pummel me. Some of her maneuvers reminded me of wrestling holds, and if I opened my eyes, I thought I might see a referee slapping the mat three times. Yes, I may have been pinned, but never had defeat felt so good.

After that, the facial was a bit of a letdown. The brochure mentioned masks of *khamin* (turmeric) and *prai* herbs, but it all felt like mud to me, and after Toey washed it off, I still had the same face. The one plus was that this procedure let me recline in a chair and observe my neighbors. One guy was having a foot massage. When I saw his eyes roll back in ecstasy, I knew Toey had saved the best for last.

She started working the wild mint lotion into my feet, and tingles shot up to my ears. When she ran a thumbnail around each of my toes, my body convulsed with pleasure.

Did I deserve such delight? Of course not. But my long-neglected feet did, and I suspected they'd be thanking me for weeks.

I emerged a new man. The path back down the mountain felt different beneath my feet. All the bumps had been rubbed away.

Meal 500: A Landmark
In the Movable Feast of Asia

SINGAPORE — We devour the Tasmanian rock oysters, attack the Canadian littleneck clams, gorge on the New Zealand green-lipped mussels and practically inhale the Norwegian cod. A second wind carries us through the scallops, tiger prawns, salmon and yabbies, crawfish-like creatures that taste like sweet prawns. Close to bursting, we plunge into the Australian lobsters.

This fresh seafood orgy is not without good reason: It isn't every day you sit down to your 500th consecutive meal on the road.

It's fitting that this milestone falls in Singapore, where Andrea and I have flown from Ko Samui, Thailand. This island city-state, located at the tip of the Malay Peninsula, is famous for its outstanding food. The venue for our 500th meal abroad is Blue Lobster, a trendy new restaurant in the Riverwalk, a complex of eateries on the Singapore River between Boat and Clarke quays. As we wrestle the mound of seafood before us, we reflect on the preceding 499 meals—the good, the bad and the unrecognizable.

On the whole, we've been impressed with the quality of fare brought to the table during the first half of our journey. On many days we've enjoyed tasty food served in spectacular settings, from the South Pacific to the Himalayas to the Gulf of Tonkin. We've even occasionally run into some good service.

For the most part, we've stuck to the local cuisine, eating chicken tikka in India, for example, or dal bhat, a lentil dish, in Nepal. This strategy produced a savory surprise a few weeks ago in Lijiang, China. We were just off the bus, tired and hungry, unwilling to forage far for food. We stumbled into a no-name street stall and sat on plastic stools at a round plastic table. The menu was in Chinese, and nobody spoke English. A man at a nearby table lifted noodles from a soup bowl with chopsticks. I pointed to the man and held up two fingers for the waitress, indicating we wanted whatever our neighbor was eating.

The cook emerged from the kitchen moments later bearing two big bowls of bubbling gray broth. On her next trip, she carried a tray of plates and bowls containing myriad ingredients: chicken pieces, raw pork slices, various greens and white noodles. I could not identify the other items: tiny raw eggs of some sort; a fleshy, ribbon-like substance; and some black wiggly things that looked like they might swim away from my chopsticks.

I figured you picked your own ingredients, but the cook dumped them all into our bowls. I watched the makings boil and simmer, then tentatively dipped a spoon into the caldron. It was delicious, one of the best meals I'd had in months. The tab for two, including tea, was less than $2. My only regret was that I did not know the name of my lunch, so I was unlikely to find it anywhere else in China.

It's not always easy to sample the native cuisine. Many restaurants on the international tourist trail play it safe with menus like those at a T.G.I. Friday's—pages and pages of selections to appeal to every palate but the local one. Not that we were looking, but we never found a restaurant in Vietnam that could pull off lasagna, beef stroganoff and tacos with equal aplomb. A general rule: the more Western the items on the menu, the less sumptuous the food. Many dishes are Western in name only. The "pizza" you spot on the menu can turn into a ketchup sandwich by the time it reaches the table.

Andrea has had a couple of memorable menu misunderstandings. At the Weilong Hotel in Kunming, China, she ordered the mushroom and bacon quiche. After a 45-minute wait, during which I finished my dinner and dessert, she was served a plate of mushroom caps sprinkled with bacon bits. Earlier on the trip, at a cafe in Nelson, New Zealand, she chose the "vege-burger," expecting a patty of soybean or mushroom. Arriving instead was a garden salad spilling from a hamburger bun.

Yet for each time we've suddenly lost our appetites, there were dozens of days our taste buds were dancing with delirium. In Jodhpur, India, Andrea discovered the lassi, a blended drink of yogurt and fresh fruit. To her delight, the creamy concoction has continued to pop up on menus across Asia.

One morning in Bangkok, we took a break from the unfamiliar. We lined up for the breakfast buffet at the 5-star

Oriental Hotel in Bangkok, served on a terrace above the Chao Phraya River. Andrea regretted that the business setting merely reminded her of work, but I was mighty impressed by the nine different fresh juices on tap. That is, until the bill ($41) arrived, at which point I considered jumping into the river and swimming away.

Beautiful scenery makes food taste better, and the trip has offered it in abundant supply. We have been lucky to dine often on or near water. We feasted on fresh fish steps from the Pacific Ocean in Fiji; enjoyed stir-fry on the banks of the pretty Perfume River in Hue, Vietnam; and savored delectable curries on moonlit rooftop restaurants overlooking romantic Lake Pichola in Udaipur, India.

Our second most time-consuming activity on this trip is eating. It's topped only by the many hours we spend waiting for the check. There must be a school in this part of the world where would-be waiters are taught to take your order, bring your food, then never again glance in your direction. I know it's rude in many countries we've visited to make the customer feel even slightly rushed, but I'd quickly forgive the waiter who established eye contact with me at least once between breakfast and closing time. There have been some interminable meals when I feared that the next person to approach our table would be a doctor—coming to check for my pulse.

Ah, but a trip around the world is no time to be watching the clock. Besides, we're adjusting to the pace. Most nights, like this one in Singapore, we're happy to linger over whatever gets served up on this movable feast.

Five hundred meals on the road sounds like a lot, but I figure we're good for 500 more.

On a Balinese Tour, Hours Fly By With the Birds

UBUD, Indonesia — I don't know a sparrow from a swallow, a crow from a crane, a loon from a lark. When I see a pretty bird, the closest I come to a scientific identification is, "Hey, look at that pretty bird!" So when I got a chance to follow an expert bird-watcher, I seized it like a hawk.

Andrea and I traded the sparkling streets of Singapore for the lush landscapes of Bali, the best known of Indonesia's 13,700 islands. Bali was always on our itinerary, but weather caused our geographical jump backward. We could have fit the island in last winter on our way from New Zealand to India, but we wanted to visit here during the dry season.

After landing in Denpasar, we headed north into the foothills to Ubud, a sprawling town and the center of Balinese art and culture. Seeking a respite from the traffic and congestion strangling this island many still call paradise, we signed up for a four-hour hike with Bali Bird Walks. The guided trek—$33 per person, lunch included—promised to put us within sight of about 30 of Bali's 300 bird species.

Our guide for the morning was Sumadi, an enthusiastic woman enthralled by birds for as long as she can recall. As a child, she accompanied her parents to work in the rice paddies, where she observed the traits and habits of the birds that soared and streaked around her. She later met Victor Mason, an English ornithologist and Bali resident who taught her the English and scientific names of the many species she had studied informally. The women of her village chide her for being unmarried at 32, but she enjoys her freedom, she said. A husband would not have allowed her to travel to the nearby island of Java to see the peacocks or to venture out for days to capture a glimpse of the endangered Bali starling, her island's only endemic bird.

Sumadi handed each of the four members of our group a pair of binoculars—devices I had previously used mainly at rock concerts and horse races—and led us up a dirt path through rice paddies fringed with coconut palms and banana trees. Almost immediately, she saw one of the more spectacular birds found on Bali, the Java kingfisher.

"Do you see it, Mike?" Sumadi asked excitedly, grabbing my arm.

I trained my binoculars on the distant darting and dipping bird, and my eyes met with a riot of color: dark brown head, cinnamon throat and breast, cobalt blue belly, purple back, light blue wings and tail, red bill and feet. Tingles shot through my limbs.

"Yes, I see it," I said, instantly grasping the thrill of birding.

Sumadi pointed overhead to three domed nests clinging to swaying palm fronds. They were the homes of streaked weavers. The gold-crowned male of the species is polygamous, but he must build a separate nest for each wife he takes. The female inspects the nest, ensuring it meets her approval, before allowing her mate to fly off in search of another companion.

When Andrea and I arrived in Bali, we were struck by the lovely aesthetics: cut fresh flowers on the bed, intricately carved garnishes on the dinner plate. That sense of decoration extends to the fields, where farmers adorn the edges of their land with flowers such as hibiscus, gloriosa lilies and stars of Bethlehem. Each day, the farmers offer some of the flowers to Dewi Sri, Hindu goddess of rice, setting them on simple wooden altars built in the rice paddies.

Our bird-watching group climbed the gentle slope, pausing to admire whatever birds flashed in view: fan-tailed warblers, Javan pond herons, scaly-breasted munias.

We descended to a small stream, where Sumadi pointed out other fauna and flora: a fire-red Malay lacewing butterfly fluttering in the shadows; a vibrant yellow and black spider spinning its web; a mimosa plant, whose feathery leaves close tight at the slightest touch. Everywhere we turned, there was some brilliant bit of nature that I would not have noticed the day before.

Back in the rice paddies, we came upon an old farmer. (Balinese farmers tend to be older; the younger generation finds it can earn more in the tourist industry.) He chopped a hole into several coconuts with a hatchet, and we each hoisted one like a bota bag, letting the sticky, clear juice spill down our throats. After the coconuts were drained, the man hacked them open, and we scooped the sweet, gelatinous meat into our mouths using pieces of its shell for spoons.

When we resumed birding, we spotted a long-tailed shrike perched atop a post. The black-masked bird of prey surveyed the field for a smaller bird it might snare with its sharp claws. The shrike would then impale its victim on a thorn, returning to peck at the bird at its leisure.

We later gazed at what I thought were two identical white birds wading in a flooded rice paddy. But a closer look revealed a slight difference: the one with the yellow bill was a cattle egret, and the black-billed one was a little egret. As the hours and birds flew by, I learned to distinguish among many of the species Sumadi had introduced us to earlier.

At the end of the bird walk, I thought of home, San Diego. We live in a neighborhood where the streets are named for birds: Dove, Goldfinch, Ibis and so on. I realized that my lesson in the birds of Bali would not help me in California. I still can't tell a bluebird from a blue jay. But if a Java kingfisher ever lands in our backyard, I'll know what to call it.

Floating Like a Butterfly
On the Swift Breezes of Bali

DAUSA, Indonesia — The day we arrived in Bali the sky was filled with kites. "There must be some big festival," I said to Andrea. But I soon learned it was another routine day in kite-crazy Bali.

Kite flying is a vital part of Balinese culture, with roots in mythology. It's believed that the deity Rare Angon, protector of crops, is most benevolent when kites ride the wind. Kites are used in religious events but are mainly flown for fun. Balinese young and old launch them from beaches, soccer fields, rice paddies, wherever they can find a path to the sky.

As we traveled the island, admiring the airborne dancers, I flashed on my youth. My heart had soared the rare times there was money for a kite. The cheap, paper ones from the supermarket cost 15 cents, a dime more for a ball of string. I'd fashion a tail out of strips cut from a tattered sheet pulled from the back of the linen closet.

I later built a kite with my grandfather out of scrap wood and newspaper. I was thrilled when that homely craft lifted from the ground. That was 30 years ago—the last time I had flown a kite.

It's a mystery how we can forget the things we enjoy. I wasn't sure why I had come to Bali, but I now had a clear reason to stay: I needed to go fly a kite.

In Ubud, the heart of Balinese arts and crafts, I found the Kites Centre, a family-run shop that makes 400 kites per month, most for export to the West. Hanging from the walls and ceiling were kites in the shapes of dragons, frogs, eagles, crabs, fish and rabbits. The hand-painted wings, from 3 to 16 feet long, were nylon, the frames bamboo and the bodies papier-mâché.

After a 30-year hiatus, I needed a kite that would be easy to get aloft. Proprietor Mang Nix suggested the butterfly, a 3-foot model with legs and antennae made from pipe cleaners. It was a flying work of art splashed with blues and greens, a little like Monet's "Water Lilies." The kite, which took a worker three 10-hour days to build, cost less than $8. That sum is beyond the reach of most Balinese kite enthusiasts, many of whom fly kites made from plastic trash bags.

We pointed our rental car to the north of the island in search of a stiff breeze.

In Dausa, a mountain village 10 miles west of the volcano Gunung Batur, I spotted a boy with a kite standing in a field on a ridge. The Bali Sea was visible far to the north; green farmland rolled down to the south. The wind bent the tall grass surrounding a Hindu temple.

Kite in hand, I tentatively approached the boy, indicating I'd like to share his airspace. He looked about 9, dressed in raggedy shorts and a too-big, stretched-out T-shirt that failed to cover one of his shoulders. He flashed me a brilliant smile beneath a runny nose and said, "Hello."

I returned the greeting, relieved I was welcome on his turf.

We stood there exchanging 10, 11, 12 "hellos."

Unable to verbally communicate further, we let our kites do the talking.

His flying Hefty bag said, "Whee! Yippee! Yee-haw!" as it screamed across the sky.

My fancy butterfly said, "Help…ugh…oops," as it struggled to leave the ground.

A crowd gathered. Pressure mounted. But each time my kite gained a bit of altitude, it crashed and cartwheeled across the field. I'd untangle the string from the butterfly's legs, pull grass from his antennae, flick mud from his head and send him up again, only to watch him spiral and plummet.

Meantime, the boy cut holes in the sky with his scrap of plastic. He flew circles around my kite in the brief moments it was aloft. He made airplane noises and pretended to attack my kite with his like a jet fighter, breaking off before a collision, laughing as I flinched.

"The kid is divebombing me," I said to Andrea, plucking the butterfly from the weeds yet again.

"Don't blame it on the child," she said. "It's unprofessional."

I tried something different: I released more string. That was it. Sometimes you just need to let go.

The kite shimmied and soared, climbing higher and higher, lifting 100 yards of string into the air. It all came back to me then, that childlike sense of awe and wonder, that exhilarating sensation of holding wings in your hands. I looked over at the boy, and he was positively beaming, sharing in the joy.

I wrote off what happened next to 30 years' lack of practice. The wind decreased, and I forgot to tug on the string. My butterfly fell to earth like a wounded duck.

The boy and I groaned. Then we laughed.

I reeled in the butterfly and stowed it in the car. I sat in the front seat, studying a map to see where I would next fly my kite.

Everyone left except the boy, who sat on a stone wall across the road from our car. His smile was gone.

When I handed him my kite, he looked confused. I had to take a step back before he knew the butterfly was now his. The brilliant smile returned to his face.

He sprinted down the road, clutching the kite, shouting with glee at everyone he passed. Every few strides, he leaped into the air, each time bounding higher, until I thought nothing could bring him down.

Playing the Hotel Game
By House Rules

PENANG, Malaysia — The sign in the hotel elevator depicted a prickly fruit inside a circle with a slash through it. "No Durians Allowed," it read.

"They smell," said the desk clerk at the Paradise Tanjung Bungah, explaining that the pungent but popular Asian fruit is unwelcome in most Malaysian hotels. "If you ate one on the first floor, you'd smell it on the third."

After a detour from Singapore east to Bali, Andrea and I had flown to this island off the northwest coast of peninsular Malaysia, resuming our westward journey around the world. Although we were unfamiliar with the durian, the hotel ban on it did not surprise us. Each new country—Malaysia is the 11th of our trip—brings a new set of house rules, amenities and nuances.

We've been lucky to sleep in some exquisite digs—from beach bungalows to mountain lodges to desert castles—all enhanced by local flavor not found at home. And even when lodging has been ordinary, like our hotel on Penang, some entertaining detail has made the stay memorable.

Some of our favorite hotels have been those where we've been allowed to observe, or even participate in, native rituals. In Jaisalmer, India, we shared the Hotel Jaisal Castle with the family that owns it. Each day, members of three generations burned incense and prayed before Hindu altars throughout the building. The hotel is built into the yellow sandstone walls of an 844-year-old fort, and our room's balcony afforded a view of the Thar Desert stretching out to the frontier of Pakistan. So aged is the structure that honey-colored ceiling chips rained down on us in the night like gold dust.

Later, in the Rajasthan city of Bikaner, we checked into the Hotel Harasar Haveli on the eve of Holi, a festival marking the end of winter. Revelers celebrate by dousing one another with water and brightly colored powders. Tourists are urged to stay indoors, as festivities can turn rowdy. But our hotel's young, exuberant owner, Bubbles, didn't want us to miss out, so he threw a Holi party in the courtyard, complete with trash cans of water and mounds of pigments. After we were sprinkled and smeared, Bubbles packed 16 guests into his pickup and drove us through town as we were bombarded with water balloons by merrymakers shouting, "Happy Holi!"

In several countries, hotels have featured niceties that seem standard issue throughout the nation. The first question we were asked in every New Zealand motel was not "Smoking or nonsmoking?" but "Full fat or skim?"—as in milk for tea. Rooms come with electric teakettles and tea bags, as well as a fridge to store your milk of choice, which is handed out at the front desk. But don't linger too long over that cuppa; the Kiwi checkout time is almost always 10 a.m.

Vietnamese hotels' ubiquitous amenity is the toothbrush. No matter how modest the room—even those with only one bedsheet—we always found two individually packaged toothbrushes on the sink. I pack light, but I doubt I'll ever consider a toothbrush too heavy to stick in my knapsack.

Our average nightly room rate thus far is $28, a figure that will jump once we reach Europe. The most we've spent is $78, for a deluxe room at the Grand Chateau in Tongariro National Park in New Zealand. The mountain resort is rich with character, but it is not our favorite to date. That spot is held by the Chomrong Guest House, in Chomrong, Nepal, where $1.80 bought a room with a panoramic view of the snowy Annapurna range.

As we seek a place to rest our heads each night, we employ two tactics we've never used at home: inspecting rooms and bargaining, both routine in this part of the world. We rarely settle for the first room we're shown; the more we look at, the better they get. At the Prince Hotel in Hanoi, $15 can put you in a cramped, windowless cell (the first we were shown) or a spacious, double-windowed room filled with antiques (the fourth).

Discounts of up to 75% have also been there for the asking. In Ubud, Bali, Andrea negotiated a $65 bungalow at the idyllic Fibra Inn down to $25, including breakfast. Our unit was fronted by a private patio with a four-poster daybed. Staff dressed in elegant sarongs glided by throughout the day to place offerings of flowers and fruit on the Hindu altars standing directly off our porch.

In China, every hotel required a cash deposit of as much as four times the nightly rate. All rooms displayed a list of prices we'd be charged if specific furnishings were damaged or stolen. At the Ming Yuan Hotel in Nanning, the mattress was listed at 900 *yuan* ($1 equals about 8 *yuan*), luggage rack 50 *yuan*, bath towel 30 *yuan*, toilet 300 *yuan*, carpet 100 *yuan* per square meter and so on. I have no idea what a "pot culture" is, but if we broke it or swiped it, we were out 30 *yuan*. The Ming Yuan also prohibited "gambling," "wrestling" and "lecherous cats."

The most memorable house rules so far (and the easiest to comply with) were at the Freedom Hotel in Siem Reap, Cambodia. The sign on our closet door read: "It is against hotel regulations to have firearms or explosives in your room without our approval."

Durians, however, were acceptable.

Part Four:

Europe

In Scotland, the Comforts of Home In an Apartment

EDINBURGH, Scotland — "I can't hear you. I'm in the other room!"

It's a familiar cry at home in San Diego. Andrea or I will be talking in the kitchen, say, oblivious that the other is in the living room. It gets old. But not last week. Each time it got hollered last week, it was a sweet reminder that we had the luxury of standing in two different rooms.

For the first time in five months, when we stayed in a condo in New Zealand, the door to our lodging opened to something other than a bed and night stand. We rented a four-room apartment in a stone building near the heart of Edinburgh, a few blocks south of the Scottish capital's medieval Old Town.

The $450-a-week flat was cheaper than most centrally located B&Bs (no easy find during the busy summer season) and offered spaciousness absent in even a posh hotel suite. The switch in our accommodation routine also let us see one of Europe's more captivating cities as locals might, frequenting neighborhood markets, shops and restaurants slightly removed from the tourist track.

We arrived here after three connecting flights from Penang, Malaysia. The 17-hour trip was the biggest leap of the journey since we left the U.S. for Fiji last January. We flew over a big chunk of the world, but after six months in the South Pacific and Asia, we know we can't see it all in one year. Besides, we've already backtracked twice on this journey—from the Indian subcontinent to Southeast Asia, and from Singapore to Bali—so our arrival in Britain doesn't rule out visits to countries we've passed. We may get to Kyrgyzstan yet.

We found the flat on the Internet at www.aboutscotland.com, one of many Web sites that popped up during a search for "self-catering accommodation in Edinburgh." A couple of mouse clicks took us to a photo album of short-term rentals. We sent a mass e-mail to the owners of about a dozen, learning that two were vacant during the third week in July. We chose a unit at 5 Buccleuch Terrace. "Third-floor apartment, ideal for couple," the Web page read. "Quiet, comfortable, modernized flat."

We were in Bali at the time, so the tricky part was prepaying the owner, Diana Harkiss, whose Web site was not set up to accept credit cards. Andrea solved the problem by walking from bank to bank in Ubud until she found one able to convert Indonesian *rupiah* into British pounds and wire them to Diana's bank in Edinburgh, an electronic transaction that took eight days to complete.

We landed in Edinburgh at 7 a.m., while other tenants were still in the flat, so Diana let us leave our backpacks at her house. She offered us coffee, drove us to the city center and said she'd carry our bags up to the flat when she went to clean it. We figured anybody this hospitable wouldn't be renting out a dump, and we were right. When we opened the door to the flat later that day, it was prettier than the pictures on the Web site.

Diana had left us a plate of chocolates and biscuits on the kitchen counter next to a bouquet of flowers. The recently remodeled apartment sparkled, boasting high ceilings, light wood floors and freshly painted white walls. The sun beamed through the tall windows of the living room, and the windows of the bedroom and dining room looked out on a sprawling, leafy tree.

The fully equipped kitchen featured a microwave, toaster and washing machine, appliances we had forgotten existed. The bathroom had fluffy new towels and ornamental glass turtles. Other homey touches included a remote-control TV, a radio and a couple of shelves of books. All the rooms were decorated with plants, nicely framed prints and Ikea furniture.

We had little to hang in the massive closets of the L-shaped hallway, but Andrea did her best.

"I want to unpack," she said, unzipping her bulging knapsack. "I want to get disorganized, then reorganized."

After settling in, we walked to the nearby Tesco supermarket to stock up on the week's provisions. We enjoyed home-cooked meals of roasted chicken and pasta, and on two nights we had pizza delivered. We liked dining in for a change, and the presence of a refrigerator meant we could graze at will. We are particularly fond of snacking on carrots and hummus while reclining on the couch. A couch! What a concept. After sitting on beds in hotel rooms for half a year, we've concluded that the couch is the most underrated of all furniture.

When we ventured out, we were delighted that Scotland was enjoying a rare warm, sunny spell. The imposing Edinburgh Castle, the tartaned and tweedy Royal Mile, and several museums were within a 20-minute walk. Closer to our apartment were bookshops, cinemas and the Meadows, an expansive swath of green that begged to be strolled. Also nearby were several newsstands and a gourmet coffee cart. I was always content to climb the three flights of stairs to our flat, a latte in one hand and a saucy tabloid in the other.

Although we planned to visit Europe, Scotland wasn't on the original itinerary. We were here last year. Our return was prompted partly by my passion for golf. It was not by chance that we rented the flat the same week the British Open golf championship was going on an hour north in the seaside town of St. Andrews. We traveled there by train and bus, amused to hear British, Irish and American golf fans attempt to communicate in English.

A year ago, as I teed off in front of the stone clubhouse of the Royal and Ancient Golf Club, my knees nearly buckled from excitement and fear. It was thrilling to again walk the links of the Old Course, where golf has been played since the 16th century. But this time I was a spectator. Seeing Jack Nicklaus play in what is expected to be his final Open and Tiger Woods complete his career Grand Slam (winning all four major championships) at the most famous golf course in the world is something I'm not likely to forget.

On another day, we rented a car and drove to North Berwick, a Victorian seaside town about 30 miles east of Edinburgh. The sweeping, sandy bay commands a glorious view of Bass Rock, a seven-acre island that is home to one lighthouse and 150,000 gannets that turn the volcanic rock white.

The beach also flanks the West Links, an ancient golf course with old stone fences crossing its fairways. It remains my favorite spot on the planet.

I know we said we'd skip destinations we had previously visited, but a benefit of wandering is wandering back to the places you love.

The end of our week in the flat came too soon. Before we knew it, we were clearing out for some other lucky travelers. We set the keys on the counter, next to the vase of flowers, and gently closed the door behind us.

It felt like we were leaving home.

Kings of the Road on the Irish Coast

ARDARA, Ireland — The road trip was a success before we even buckled up.

National Car Rental in Belfast, Northern Ireland, honored the erroneous low price we were quoted on the Internet, allowing us to drive off in a $750-a-week car for $155, insurance and one-way drop fee included.

"I'd like to get a car at that rate," said the befuddled clerk.

The savings meant we could afford gas, currently fetching $6 per gallon in Britain.

After leaving our rented flat in Edinburgh, Scotland, Andrea and I traveled by train and ferry to Belfast. We then drove for four days across the top of Northern Ireland and Ireland—from the Irish Sea to the North Atlantic—touring a part of the Emerald Isle we missed on a trip here three years ago. The call of the road in Ireland, with its promise of wild headlands, rugged mountains and mystical bogs, is not easily ignored.

We rolled north out of Belfast, Andrea at the wheel of our Vauxhall Vectra, the British version of a Chevrolet. Near the coastal village of Ballintoy, we stopped to traverse the Carrick-a-Rede rope bridge, spanning 80 feet above the ocean, from the mainland to a small island that gives fishermen access to migrating salmon. A few miles west, we pulled over to scramble across the geological phenomenon known as the Giant's Causeway, a stretch of mostly hexagonal stone columns, some as tall as 40 feet, packed tightly and extending into the sea.

Northern Ireland offers the same sublime scenery as its larger Irish neighbor, but without the snarl of tour buses.

"We don't get many tourists in Northern Ireland," said Peter Pyne, owner of the Saddler's House, a bed-and-breakfast in Derry, the country's second largest city. "They're frightened to come here."

Fears about the sectarian violence so quaintly called "the Troubles" means it's easy to get a dinner reservation. We strolled to an upscale bistro Pyne recommended as police vans that looked like armored tanks cruised the quiet streets. Two young men urinating outside the restaurant window while we ate added to the menacing atmosphere.

Although the country is as safe as others we've visited, tensions were high. The week we were there, more than 80 Republican and Loyalist terrorists were released from prison as part of the Good Friday peace accord.

"There'll never be peace," said an old man feeding pigeons atop the 17th century wall circling central Derry. "You can't make peace with murderers."

We encountered a lighter tone in the seaside resort town of Portstewart, where we secured the road trip's missing ingredient—music—by buying CDs by Bob Dylan, Jimi Hendrix, Steve Earle and Moby. But the musical find of the day came half an hour later in a shopping center parking lot hosting a "boot sale," a flea market where people sell stuff out of the trunks of their cars. From the clutter of old toys, clothing, tools and Christmas gnomes, I plucked a mint-condition CD by Latin vocal stylist Trini Lopez, adding that degree of hilarity demanded by any serious road trip. We barreled west into County Donegal, Ireland, snapping fingers to Trini's swinging rendition of "If I Had a Hammer."

Ever since our first trip to Ireland, we've fantasized about spending a couple of weeks here in a thatch-roofed cottage overlooking the sea. There was no time for that on this trip, but we were lucky to find vacant a stone cottage at the Green Gate, a B&B perched on a hill above Ardara, a coastal hamlet known for its tweeds and wool sweaters.

The cottage, bordered by red, yellow and green fishing-net buoys, has an antique iron stove for a nightstand and a seashell sconce for a reading light. Compensating for the low ceiling are the windows, positioned so that guests reclining in bed or the bathtub can gaze out at Loughros More Bay and, beyond that, the Atlantic Ocean.

That night, we enjoyed the best meal of the journey, the fresh seafood platter at Nancy's, a tiny pub that has been in the same family for seven generations.

In the morning we ate breakfast in the Green Gate's cozy main house, where the colorful French owner, Paul Chatenoud, regaled guests with stories while stoking the peat fire. He proudly displayed a thick guest book stuffed with poems, songs and sketches penned in tribute to the B&B. A Canadian at the table mentioned that her guidebook said Paul is as charming as the Green Gate. Paul chuckled and said, "But that was 10 years ago."

Paul, who formerly ran a bookstore in Paris, unfolded a map and showed us his favorite drive in Ireland, a loop around the nearby Slieve League peninsula. Following his directions, we headed west along a lonely one-lane road. Sheep, tagged with bright spray paint to identify them to their owners, meandered in our path. Streams tumbled down rock-strewn mountains. Stone fences scaled green hillsides. The occasional palm tree in the mist looked like a mirage.

We pulled onto a dirt track that ended at the base of a peak. We left the car and climbed for an hour.

At the top, what little breath we had left was taken away by the view. We stared straight down at the ocean, about 2,000 feet below. We were standing alone atop Slieve League, among Europe's highest sea cliffs. Halfway down the cliff, sea gulls soared. I turned from the edge without blinking, holding the picture in my mind.

We walked back down the mountain to the car, returning to the road and the hope of wonders to come.

The Latest Chapter
In a Journey Brightened by Books

HAY-ON-WYE, Wales — With more than 1 million books for sale in about 30 bookshops, including one in a 13th century castle, this tiny town on the border of Wales and England is known as the secondhand book capital of the world. Visitors who browse the musty stone buildings lining the old, narrow streets will find entire shelves of books on such slender subjects as Himalayan kingdoms, Eskimos, land mines and Bulgarian history.

When Andrea and I arrived from Ireland in this charming hamlet on the River Wye, we were reminded of how much of our journey we've spent hunting, trading and reading books, often in places where they are hard to find. Aside from the pleasure of passing the hours and miles with a good book, reading about the countries we've visited has also enriched our travels.

Andrea is the reader between the two of us, and our trip has let her do more of what she already does a lot of at home. I'm embarrassed to admit that the large chunk of time I spend in the States playing golf and watching it on TV makes my library card a waste of plastic. But stripped of my clubs and remote control, I suddenly have time to dive into something deeper than *Golf Digest*.

Early on in this journey, my goal was to read a book about each upcoming country on our itinerary. While touring New Zealand, I was amazed by *Midnight's Children*, Salman Rushdie's novel of modern India, and in India, I was entranced by *The Snow Leopard*, Peter Matthiessen's account of his spiritual sojourn to the Dolpo region of Nepal. My plan fell apart in Nepal, where I couldn't find any titles on Vietnam, the next country we traveled at length.

I turned to books I should have read long ago, such as Joseph Conrad's *Heart of Darkness* and John Steinbeck's *East of Eden*. Meanwhile, Andrea was reading everything I had and knocking off such classics as Thomas Hardy's *Far From the Madding Crowd*, J.R.R. Tolkien's *Lord of the Rings* and Leo Tolstoy's *War and Peace*. Finishing the 1,444-page Tolstoy tome left room in her pack for five average-sized novels, and we were off and reading.

We trade books in as we go, usually exchanging two of our used paperbacks for one of the vendor's. We occasionally get the chance to trade for goods other than books. In Yangshuo, China, a restaurateur offered us pork fried rice for Arthur Golden's *Memoirs of a Geisha*, which we declined because we had already eaten and were about to board a bus. At a shop in Marpha, Nepal, a village in the Annapurna mountain range where everything is carried up on the backs of humans or donkeys, we swapped our dog-eared copy of *The Snow Leopard* for three rolls of toilet paper, certain we got the better end of the deal.

We saw few English-language bookstores on the backpacker trail in Asia—Kathmandu, Nepal, being the exception—but found many cafes and guest houses that sell books on the side. As these places rely on trade-ins for stock, we were limited to the literary tastes of travelers before us. Shelves sagged under multiple copies of thrillers by such best-selling authors as John Grisham and Tom Clancy, books we've so far resisted. But from the popular heap, we've seized more engaging fare, including Charles Frazier's *Cold Mountain*, Tom Wolfe's *A Man in Full*, Bernard Malamud's *A New Life* and several installments from P.G. Wodehouse's *Jeeves* series.

It was tough finding English-language books in China, where there are strong censorship laws. We also had trouble keeping up with news of the world. We saw no foreign newspapers, and the Internet sites for the *Los Angeles Times* and other American media are blocked by the government.

Most of the books sold to travelers in Vietnam are photocopies. Peddlers walk from cafe to cafe hawking the same armload of titles, including Arundhati Roy's *The God of Small Things*, Jung Chang's *Wild Swans* and several Lonely Planet guidebooks. I was thrilled to spot Michael Herr's *Dispatches*, a book I'd searched for since India. Herr's saga of his stint as a war correspondent in Vietnam was so gripping, I felt doubly guilty that none of the $4 I paid for the bootlegged book would find its way to the author.

Whether reading on the beach in Thailand, in a mountain hut in New Zealand or on a train crossing the Ganges Plain of India, I've yet to meet a book on this trip I didn't like. A benefit of limited selection is that you're exposed to books you might not otherwise read. After finishing Graham Greene's *The Quiet American*, a novel set in 1950s Vietnam, and Robertson Davies' mysterious and mystical *The Cunning Man*, I felt silly for not having read these authors before, and I've been on the lookout for their works ever since.

Before we left home, Andrea's aunt, Betty Fraser, mentioned Richard Halliburton, an adventurer and author popular in the 1920s and '30s. Halliburton was a favorite of Betty's late father (Andrea's grandfather), C.S. Boyles Jr., who penned Western novels and short stories under the name Will C. Brown. Eager to learn what captivated her grandfather, Andrea tracked down one of Halliburton's out-of-print books, *The Flying Carpet*, an account of his journey around most of the world in an open-cockpit plane. When we reached Fiji, we delighted in reading about Halliburton's exploits, such as swimming in the pool outside the Taj Mahal and hanging with headhunters in Borneo.

In Hay-on-Wye, our three-day search through the endless stacks turned up five copies of Halliburton's travelogues—two each of *The Royal Road to Romance* and *New Worlds to Conquer*, and a signed first edition of *The Glorious Adventure*. We paid $27 for the books and shipped them home. Our journey may end in December, but with Halliburton, we can continue traveling from the armchairs of our living room.

Over Hill and Dale in Cotswolds

BATH, England — Three horses blocked our path through the gate, ignoring my stomping, waving and bellowing. I pulled out the miniature key-ring harmonica I'd recently bought in Ireland. I'm no musician, so it was by accident that I blew a sweet and lonesome cowboy tune, only piquing the horses' interest and drawing them nearer. My lips raced over the tiny harp until they locked onto a screeching note, sending the horses trotting in another direction, leaving us to continue our hike.

Andrea and I had negotiated the latest obstacle along the Cotswold Way, a 104-mile trail in western England that runs roughly north to south, from the engaging town of Chipping Campden to the historic city of Bath. The route combines footpaths, bridle ways and minor roads to carry the hiker along the western edge of the Cotswolds, a belt of limestone hills overlooking the Evesham and Severn valleys and the distant rolling land of Wales. The trail wends across green pastures, wooded hollows and wind-swept plateaus, frequently dipping into quaint hamlets studded with buildings of Cotswold stone, a creamy yellow rock that glows on even the cloudiest of days. It's a demanding walk, but in the week it took us to finish, we were rewarded with some of the most glorious scenery the English countryside has to offer.

We trekked 10 to 20 miles per day, staying at B&Bs along the way. We were in Singapore when we decided to take the walk, so we paid $85 to the Internet site www.cotswold-way.co.uk to book our lodgings. For $105 more, the site arranged to transport our bags daily to our next stop. Most nights, we ate in pubs near our bed-and-breakfasts, and on days when we wouldn't pass a restaurant by noon, our hosts sent us off with sack lunches.

We had already taken challenging hikes in New Zealand and Nepal earlier on this journey, and we weren't expecting much of a test from the Cotswolds. I thought hiking is to England what skiing is to Nebraska, but the Cotswold Way is deceiving. Although the hills barely rise above 1,000 feet, the trail goes down and up so much that the aggregate climb is close to 13,000 feet. The path is often muddy and cut by horse hoofs. It's also dotted by 225 stiles, most requiring the hiker to step up and over fences, so you soon feel like a contestant in a grueling steeplechase. We didn't trudge into the first night's stop of Winchcombe until after dark, and I nearly cried when the B&B owner told us our room was upstairs.

No matter how sore we woke each morning, the idyllic route usually returned the spring to our step. The trail would meander by grazing sheep, lead us across a churchyard, guide us through a forest of beech and deposit us next to a field of poppies so red it looked like it was afire. As dusk fell on the hamlet of Hailes one day, we passed crumbling cloister arches, all that remain of the 13th century Hailes Abbey. The next day, the path took us by the Neolithic burial mound of Belas Knap.

England's traditional rights of way meant we were often crossing private property, traipsing through crop fields and driveways. In Little Sodbury, the trail spit us out into someone's backyard. Family members paid no notice, continuing to tend their gnome-flanked garden.

We were mostly pleased with our lodgings. In Chipping Campden, Weston Park Farm's one and only room is an entire wing of a centuries-old, ivy-covered stone farmhouse. Out one window, we watched Zodiac, the family's pet peacock, and out another, we glimpsed a red fox. At Langett B&B, outside the city of Cheltenham, we played on the floor with the owners' four Jack Russell terriers—Biff, Becka, Blossom and Freddie. In the village of Old Sodbury, we slept at Dornden Guest House, a former vicarage where we enjoyed a game of croquet, too pooped to use the grass tennis court.

Although it's summer, we ran into few people on the trail. One day, an older farmer fixing a stone fence on his land offered a hearty "Jolly good!" when we told him we were hiking the whole route. A few days later, we crossed paths with a man walking two Labs. During a half-hour discourse, he touched on no fewer than 20 topics, including British military aviation, the American Civil War, forensic science, Libya, the Los Angeles River and Rock Hudson. We gradually edged away. Undaunted but apparently out of segues, the man extended his arm at chest level and called after us, "The Queen Mother is only this tall!"

Each day, we had to walk more than the official distance because food and lodging were rarely on the trail. We added more miles by getting lost. The path is fairly well marked, but signs would vanish and we'd find ourselves wandering in a field bordered by barbed wire. This usually happened late in the day in a driving rain.

By midweek, I felt like I had a broken foot. We took a rest day, traveling to the next stop by bus. I foolishly resumed the hike the following morning, refusing to believe that what I thought was a gentle stroll in the country had so thoroughly whipped me.

By the time we reached Bath, a city known for its Roman baths and Georgian architecture, I was limping, and I knew I should have saddled up one of those horses instead of scaring them off with my harmonica. I touched Bath Abbey, the end of the Cotswold Way, and hobbled off to bed, vowing to never again underestimate the hills of England.

Putting the Squeeze
On a Frugal Budget in Britain

LONDON — When we entered Room 4A of the Arran House Hotel in the Bloomsbury section of this city, we thought we'd been handed the key to the storage closet.

The twin beds ran headboard to headboard the length of one wall. The floor space between them and the opposing armoire and dresser was wide enough to set our bags but not our feet. We couldn't close the door without catching a bedspread in the jamb. The remote to the tiny TV was tethered to the wall by a short leash, requiring us to stand by the door to change channels.

The narrow room wasn't all bad: The proximity of the sink meant we could brush our teeth from bed.

The wackiest part of this bathroom-less sliver of space was its nightly rate of $84—the most we've spent for accommodation on this journey. I would've raised my hands to my mouth in mock horror had there been room to bend my elbows.

After walking the Cotswold Way, Andrea and I came to London to see the sights and make onward travel plans. We were stunned to learn that the most popular tourist attractions here are no longer Buckingham Palace, the Tower of London and Big Ben, but ATMs.

The UK and Ireland have never been bargain destinations. But on this swing through the British Isles—after several months in affordable Asia—we've been astonished at how little we get for our money. The strong American dollar is a myth here, and the name of the tune this summer is "Cruel Britannia."

We felt the bite the moment we landed a month ago in Edinburgh, Scotland. The view outside the taxi window was captivating, but what really took my breath was the meter, its numbers spinning like the wheels of a Vegas slot machine. The fare for the quick eight-mile ride from the airport to the city center was $30, a sharp contrast to the $6, 30-mile trip from our hotel to the airport in Penang, Malaysia, the day before.

The United Kingdom may be small, but it costs a pretty pence to navigate it. A subway ticket in London runs $2.25. The one-way train fare from London to Hereford—about the same distance as Los Angeles to San Diego—costs $63, and that may only buy you standing room. With gas at $6 per gallon, it took $100 to fill the tank of our rental car in Northern Ireland. The bus is no bargain, either. When my foot was too sore for me to walk the Cotswold Way one day, I paid $6 to ride a bus 12 miles. It might have hurt less to crawl.

When the check arrives in restaurants, we're shocked that the tip alone amounts to more than some of our favorite meals in Asia. It's nothing to drop $60 on a forgettable dinner for two—no wine or cocktails—a dry piece of fish, say, accompanied by vegetables boiling since the Thatcher years.

This is often served by a staff whose regard for you ranges from total indifference to naked disdain.

The distress of dining is compounded by communication problems. English, a language that has served us well in a dozen other countries, is failing us now that we're in England.

The gap between price and value in this region is most striking when it comes to lodging. Guesthouse owners who learned that not everyone likes sharing a bathtub with a bunch of strangers have wedged private facilities into many of their rooms, creating some absurd living spaces. At Ashford Manor in Galway, Ireland, we paid $82 for a room with a shower stall set next to the door like a see-through closet. As the room was in what I guessed had been an attic, the encroaching pitch of the roof forced me to shower leaning sideways, my face pressed against the glass. I had to assume a similar stance in the bathroom.

Andrea and I disagreed over the virtues of the Bear B&B in Hay-on-Wye, Wales, where we paid $66 for a room without private bath. Andrea kept talking of the centuries-old stone structure's beauty and charm, qualities I apparently missed while bent over at the waist to clear the doorway. To me, the room was like a jail cell with dainty wallpaper. I flinched when I rolled over in bed, fearing I might bang my shoulder on the ceiling.

Aside from lodging, food and transportation, it's the high cost of incidentals over here that also keeps me checking my pockets for holes. A daily paper in Ireland costs $1.50. It's $5 to run a load of laundry in Bath, England. You can't always avoid the 30-cent pay toilets in London. A peek inside

Westminster Abbey will set you back $7.50. A ticket to a movie in one of the theaters around Leicester Square is $12.25, a sum that makes you feel more like a producer than a patron.

We expected Britain to break our budget, not obliterate it. Our expenses over the past month are close to $200 per day, nearly three times our target daily world average.

The thriftiest day of our journey to date was March 7, in Jaipur, India. I remember the day well. We had a large, sunny room with private bath, and a balcony affording a view of peacocks. We ate three tasty meals, rode in a rickshaw, toured a temple, gaped at elephants and monkeys and bought a few postcards. I also made it to bed without hitting my head on the doorway. Total expenses: $19.

A truism of travel, as of life in general, is that you don't know what you've got 'til it's gone.

Oh, India, how I miss you!

In Ávila,
Relearning Español Essentials

ÁVILA, Spain — Like any language, Spanish punishes imprecision. Take the word for ham: *jamón*. Get one letter wrong and order a *sandwich de jabón*, and the waiter will look at you funny or bring you a soap sandwich.

As finding something edible several times a day is a key part of world travel, Andrea and I were motivated to study Spanish. After leaving London, we enrolled in a two-week course at the Instituto Español Murallas de Ávila, a small school in this city about 70 miles northwest of Madrid. Eight months of gallivanting had prompted us to tackle a task more productive than filling our passports with visas. We also figured that whatever Spanish we learned would help us in other countries we may visit, not to mention back home in California.

We found the school through the Internet (www.iema.com), choosing it for its location and intimate, relaxed teaching style. At 3,700 feet, Ávila enjoys pleasant summers while most of the rest of Spain bakes. The old quarter of the city, birthplace of the 16th century mystic St. Teresa, is ringed by one of the best-preserved medieval walls in Europe.

Classes of three to seven students meet in an old house in the pedestrian area of town. Saddles, yokes and pitchforks hang from interior walls that surround a patio. Students are mainly from Europe and the U.S., ranging from teenagers to senior citizens. Tuition works out to less than $7 an hour.

Andrea and I last took Spanish in college 20 years ago, learning enough to ask simple questions but not enough to understand the answers. In Ávila, we overestimated our previous studies and joined an intermediate class. It was like learning to in-line skate before learning to walk, but it was loads of fun. Andrea, not usually a morning person, practically skipped to school each day down the cobblestone streets.

We attended Monday through Friday, 9 a.m. to 1:30 p.m. Our teachers, Jose-Luís, Ester and Gloria, possessed boundless energy and kept classes lively. Rather than the boring exercises of my youth ("My name is Mike. I am from San Diego"), we discussed topics such as crime and nuclear weapons.

Our limited Spanish made our solutions to world problems superficial, yet entertaining. Andrea got a big laugh the day we talked about the environment, confusing the word for grandmother (*abuela*) with the word for tree (*árbol*), telling the class she recycles her grandmother every Christmas.

Many students rent rooms from local families. The hosts we were assigned were nice, but they smoked and their apartment was a 40-minute walk from school. After one night there, we moved inside the city walls to the Hosteria las Cancelas, one of our favorite hotels so far. The small inn sits on a narrow lane once known as Calle de la Muerte y la Vida—Death and Life Street—the place where men would come to settle disputes with swords. Our large, sunny, $47 double room had a terra-cotta tile floor and an exposed brick wall. The view from the balcony took in the nearby 13th century cathedral, atop which migrating white storks build nests 2 feet tall.

We eventually adjusted to the Spanish clock, eating lunch at 3, dinner at 10. Every morning we'd join classmates and teachers for coffee in one of the cafes lining the adjacent Plaza de la Victoria. The teachers were generous with their time, offering restaurant and travel tips, and often inviting us out with their friends for *tapas*, the snacks served in most any bar in Spain.

Ester introduced us to Elena, a court reporter, and Ángel, a nurse, who were preparing for their final exams at a local English school. We met the pair several afternoons for chats, them practicing their English, us our Spanish. Our conversational skills improved, and it was a treat to talk to ordinary people not involved in the tourist industry.

Toward the end of our program I had a breakthrough. We stayed in to study one night, and I made my first phone call in Spanish, ordering out for a pizza. The deliveryman arrived, and I swelled with pride when I saw that he carried a pizza topped with ham and not soap.

I looked at the juicy, messy pie and thought it a pity I'd yet to learn the word for napkins.

Learning About Courage
And Beauty From the Beast

MADRID — I got ballet the first time I went. I didn't get bullfighting until my sixth go. My grasp of both came on a recent visit to Spain's capital.

Andrea and I had the weekend off from Spanish school in Ávila. To maximize our time, we took the 90-minute train to Madrid on Friday afternoon and returned early Monday morning before class. We ate our way through several *tapas* bars, sipped *café con leche* on the Plaza Mayor, strolled through the sprawling flea market El Rastro, and popped into the Museo Reina Sofia to view Picasso's famous painting, "Guernica."

But the highlights of the jaunt were the ballet and the bullfight.

The National Ballet of Cuba was at the Teatro Albéniz. My resistance to ballet has been so strong that Andrea asked whether I was sure I wanted to go even as we were buying the tickets. I always thought the ballet was for people with closets full of tuxedos and gowns. I also assumed you had to be an expert to enjoy it.

It's fitting that the company performed *Carmen*, much of which is set in and around a bullring. When the curtain went up, I shifted in my seat, expecting to be bored. But I was taken by the story of the gypsy Carmen and her ill-fated affair with the soldier Don José. I was dazzled by the dancers, the costumes, the music of Georges Bizet, and far from dragging, the evening passed too soon.

It hit me that you don't need to be an expert to appreciate ballet. It didn't matter that I don't know the names of the steps and jumps, or that I had never heard of Alicia Alonso, the company's director and one of the legends of dance. All that mattered was that I could finally recognize ballet as this beautiful blend of art and athleticism. Had I skipped *Rocky V* or passed on my 37th Grateful Dead concert, I might have had time for this epiphany much earlier in life.

The next day, we took the Metro to the Plaza de Toros de Las Ventas, the largest bullring in the world. The jostling crowd and the buzz of anticipation reminded me of riding the subway to Yankee Stadium when we lived in New York.

We plopped rented cushions on the third row of concrete seats in the *sol y sombra* (sun and shade) section of the arena. A few rows in the adjacent, pricier shady section were filled with Japanese tourists, many looking nervous about what they might soon see. Spaniards seated around us smoked cigars and drank whiskey; a few chatted on cellphones.

I had seen five previous bullfights (two with Andrea) in other cities in Spain and in Mexico. Madrid is the major league of the *corrida* (bullfight), so I expected something grand, but it was the same. The stands were mostly empty, and spectators didn't display the passion common at international soccer matches.

The first two bullfights on this day's card went to form: The bull charges into the ring, where after a brief encounter with the matador, he meets the picador, a man on horseback who plunges a lance between the bull's shoulders. The bleeding animal now faces the banderilleros, who take turns jabbing colorfully adorned prods into the bull's back. The matador returns with a *muleta* (red cloth) he uses to maneuver the bull around him in various passes. At the fatal moment, the matador sinks his sword into the back of the bull's neck, piercing the lungs. A brass band strikes up a festive tune as the carcass is dragged off.

The third matador of the day was Rodolfo Núñez, the best on the card, and he drew a 1,100-pound bull named Avispado, the Spanish word for "smart" or "clever." Núñez worked close enough for the bull to smear blood on the matador's *traje de luces* (suit of lights).

"Think the blood comes out of his pants?" I asked Andrea.

"Cold water," she said.

On one pass, Avispado turned his head from the *muleta*, catching Núñez with his horns and flinging him into the air. The matador landed in the dirt and covered up, the bull stomping and horning him.

Núñez's assistants rushed in to distract the bull with their capes. Núñez scrambled to his feet, limping and bleeding from his hand. He angrily waved off his helpers and aligned himself with the bull for the kill. The sword deeply buried in Avispado, Núñez stood before the faltering bull, fixing him with enraged eyes, taunting him with words and pointing at him, until the animal collapsed. As a helper stabbed the bull in the base of the skull to finish him off, the matador arched his back, posturing and preening.

But like a character in a scary movie who isn't dead when you think he is, Avispado somehow sprang to life. The bull struggled to his feet and lurched at Núñez. The matador, rattled and embarrassed, stalked the stumbling bull about the ring, at turns mocking and scolding him. When Avispado halted near the perimeter, Núñez sat on the foot railing circling the inside of the wooden fence and crossed his legs, pretending to share a park bench with the bull.

Avispado summoned a surge of energy to chase the matador away. Núñez's face was flushed, his hair mussed, and he didn't look so pretty anymore.

I glanced over to see most of the Japanese tourists had left. The bull tottered on wobbly legs along the fence below me, refusing to go down. I have heard about the will to live, but now I witnessed it. Blood poured from Avispado's nose and mouth, and his haunting bellows echoed through the stands. At last, his knees buckled, and he toppled—to my shame.

If anyone had ever asked why I occasionally went to a bullfight, I might have feebly alluded to culture, tradition, artistry and courage. But rather than reasons, these were excuses to view a spectacle I deemed at heart to be cruel and ugly. Bullfighting is not of my culture. Other barbaric traditions have been set aside. And there are many art forms and tests of courage that don't involve the contrived slaughter of animals.

I felt sick for Avispado, and I felt sick for myself. I had a cheap seat, but it was an expensive ticket.

I'll leave it to others to argue whether there is a place in the modern world for the bullfight; all I know is that the bullfight is no place for me.

Next time, I'll stick to the ballet.

Tallying Close Encounters
Of the Memorable Kind

GRANADA, Spain — I was excited to see the Alhambra again. When I toured the Moorish fortress-palace complex here in 1991, it became my favorite site in the world. Not until my recent return visit did I realize I had forgotten what the Alhambra looked like.

My enduring memory of that first trip to this city in southern Spain is of my traveling companions: Greg, from England, and Karen, from Canada. We had met on a train the day before, each boarding at a different stop, each heading for Granada and a peek at one of Islam's great works of architecture.

Greg carried a pair of skis, an oddity on the dry Andalusian plains. He was returning from a fruitless search for October snow in the High Atlas Mountains of Morocco. The three of us shared a hotel room, a couple of meals and a lot of laughs. We parted less than 24 hours later. Whenever I've fondly recalled the Alhambra, I've really been remembering the good time I had with Greg and Karen. I'd recognize them anywhere, but I couldn't pick out the architectural jewel we strolled through from a one-postcard lineup.

As Andrea and I have wandered the world, we've toured countless castles, cathedrals, temples and ruins. Yet my memory of these historic sticks and stones somehow grows fuzzy before I even toss the ticket stubs. The pictures I instead paste into my mental photo album are of the people we encounter at these sites. The edifices may fade, but the faces linger.

The most stunning site so far on this journey is the group of temples at Angkor, Cambodia, built by the Khmer civilization between the ninth and 13th centuries. Already the awesome and eerie structures have blurred in my brain, but I vividly recall our guide, Phirum Proeun, an articulate and engaging man with a quick smile.

We were in Angkor Wat, the grandest temple, when I asked about his family. He told us his father was an army officer killed by the Khmer Rouge. Proeun hacked the back of his neck with his hand to show where the machete had struck. It's an image I'm unlikely to forget.

The Taj Mahal is one of the most famous spots in the world, but our visit there was eclipsed by a brief exchange outside with an elegant Indian woman. Andrea and I were standing near the reflecting pool when the woman offered to take our picture. She was a businesswoman who had met President Clinton on his stop in Agra, India, a day earlier. The captivating woman shared her passion for the Taj with us and suggested other sites. It was refreshing to speak with someone who wasn't trying to sell us something, and she was one of the few women we met during a month in India. The Taj was a bit of a letdown, and I was sorry the woman was gone when we came out.

In the village of Ranakpur, India, we wandered into a 600-year-old Jain temple teeming with tour groups. A bearded man in a white robe and brown socks rushed up to us, panting.

"From which country?" he asked us.

"The United States," Andrea replied.

"I am the high priest of the temple," the man said. "I'm out of breath. All this meditating. My world. Your group? How many in your group?"

"Just us," I said.

"So you have no guide?" he huffed. "You are seeing individually?"

We nodded, yes.

"I see," he said. "See you later."

The high priest whirled and hurried off. Andrea and I were dumbfounded.

But the holy man was back moments later, a few other sightseers in tow. Like a good party host who wanted his guests to have a good time, he gathered all the independent travelers for a private tour. He smudged sandalwood paste on our foreheads for good luck and shared the stories behind many of the 1,444 hand-carved marble pillars that support the temple.

Every couple minutes, he'd pause his narration and interject, breathlessly: "I'm a very busy man. I only got five hours of sleep last night."

Many months later, I've largely forgotten the renowned temple, but not its panting priest. Almost daily, I turn to

Andrea and declare: "I'm a very busy man. I only got *five minutes* of sleep last night."

My pattern of drawing blanks on famous buildings while fixing on the people who frequent them is nothing new. I've been to the Louvre in Paris twice, but I doubt I could tell it from the Palace of Versailles. Andrea and I last toured the great museum three years ago, on a November weekday morning. The doors had just opened, and we found ourselves standing alone before the Mona Lisa. Suddenly two young, presumably American, women rushed up, as if on roller skates. They had big hair, frosted lipstick, nails out to here and coats with fake fur-fringed hoods. They paused long enough to each squeeze off a photo of the painting with their matching yellow disposable cameras. Then they bolted from the ornate room all shrieks and giggles, bubble-gum breath wafting behind. Ever since, it's been impossible to hear of the Louvre and not picture those women.

We briefly returned to France on this journey. After Spanish language school, we met my sister, Debbie, in Bilbao, then drove through the Basque country and the Pyrenees. One day we made a wrong turn and ended up in Lourdes, France, where the Virgin Mary is said to have appeared to St. Bernadette 18 times.

I was unimpressed by the church but taken by the stream of mainly infirm and aged faithful who venture there to douse themselves with water from the reputedly healing sacred spring. We were walking down a steep concrete ramp when I heard what I mistook as a yell of pure ecstasy. The old woman went by us in a flash, her wheelchair hurtling down the ramp, an even older woman desperately clinging to the handle grips, sprinting to keep up in high-heeled shoes. The ramp ended at a short railing. Beyond that, a 30-foot drop to the pavilion below.

I saw the tragedy before it happened, but at the last instant the wheelchair inexplicably turned left and halted. Had we witnessed the unseen hand of St. Bernadette? Who knows? But it will be a miracle if I ever erase that scene from my mind.

Some memorable encounters occur in the great outdoors. In New Zealand, we hiked the Milford Track, known as "The Finest Walk in the World." Yes, the alpine peaks, waterfalls, rain forest and fjords were pretty. But what really left an impression were the fun-loving people who joined us on the trek: a group of Kiwi women, including a champion roller skater; several Europeans; a few young Israeli guys just out of the army; a Japanese auto mechanic; and our friends, John and Lauren, from San Diego.

We bedded down each night in a series of crowded, co-ed bunkhouses along the trail. John and the Israelis were dubbed "the lumberjacks" because of the logs they sawed in their sleep. One night, when their snore fest threatened to blow the roof off our hut, John's wife, Lauren, called out to me in the dark: "Mike, if that's John, rub his chest and he'll stop." I laughed until dawn.

Later in the year, friends Chris and Mary Frances, of Los Angeles, joined us for a driving tour of Ireland. We detoured to view the Burren, a haunting limestone landscape in County Clare. Although there were few places to turn, we still got lost. I sort of remember the look of the lunar terrain. Much more vivid was the look on our faces when we passed the same road sign for the fourth time that day. A long way to Tipperary, indeed.

My favorite image thus far came in Nepal. We took a taxi from Kathmandu to the nearby town of Patan to see a temple. In the shadow of the crumbling temple, two boys played table tennis on a cement table painted green. Instead of a net, they hit the ball back and forth over a line of bricks laid end to end. I don't recall the name of the temple or whether it was Hindu or Buddhist, but my mental snapshot of the boys and their ingeniously improvised net will stay with me forever.

That's how I travel: I forget the buildings but remember the bricks.

Part Five:

North Africa

Some Postcards
From a Moroccan Carpet Ride

MARRAKECH, Morocco — We had barely arrived when we encountered Morocco's famous hospitality.

Andrea and I were riding the train from the seaport of Casablanca to this ancient city in the middle of the country. We had flown across the Mediterranean Sea from Spain, and after two months in Europe it was good to again be somewhere exotic.

A smiling bear of a man, dressed neatly in slacks and a shirt, plopped down next to me, and we chatted for much of the four-hour trip to Marrakech.

Abdellatif was returning from Rabat, the capital, where he'd been on business. He said he worked for the government, exporting Moroccan handicrafts directly to consumers. The program eliminates the middleman, he said, keeping profits in the hands of artisans. Hearing we were from California, he said his agency had clients in Palm Springs, and that he had traveled there to consult on interior design jobs.

Before boarding the train, Andrea and I had phoned ahead for a hotel reservation, but our top choices were full. Abdellatif suggested a mid-range hotel that he knew we'd prefer to the one we had settled for. He told us to pay no more than $2 for the taxi there, named a good restaurant and warned us against pickpockets. We felt lucky to meet such a helpful, English-speaking local.

Abdellatif had a wife and baby daughter in Marrakech. If we were still in town the following Friday, he said, we were invited to their house for couscous. Then, as the train pulled into the red-colored city, he asked us to join him for breakfast the next day. We quickly agreed.

Andrea and I dined that night at Argana, the rooftop cafe Abdellatif had recommended. We looked down on the Jema al-Fna, the medina's main square, where snake charmers, fire eaters, musicians and acrobats compete for coins. I instantly liked Morocco—its dreamy landscapes, its trippy vibe, its people who hold hand to heart and say, "Welcome."

Only one thing bothered me.

I caught myself questioning Abdellatif's motives. Suspicion has become second nature on this trip. When someone tries to befriend me, especially in poorer countries, I assume he's working an angle. Sadly, I've learned that this mistrust is usually warranted.

But I have my baloney radar turned up so high that I can't tell when an authentic cultural exchange is unfolding. I had no reason to suspect Abdellatif. His travel tips were good; he gave no hint of wanting a thing from us. Why couldn't his invitations to breakfast and his house be a simple gesture of goodwill?

It was a struggle, but I went to bed believing he deserved my trust. Sleep was slow to come as I wondered how I'd turned so cynical.

Abdellatif had said the breakfast place was hard to find, so we met at a cafe on the square. I felt guilty about my earlier doubts as soon as I saw him. He rose from the table, beaming, shook our hands and patted me on the shoulder. He introduced us to a government colleague, Ayub, who would lead us to the restaurant; Abdellatif would join us shortly.

We followed Ayub into the souk, a maze of twisting alleys lined with shops, crafts dealers and food stalls. Deep inside the labyrinth, he abruptly turned right.

There's a scene in "Goodfellas" when the mobster played by Joe Pesci thinks he's being escorted to the Mafia ceremony that will make him a made man, but instead he gets whacked. When he realizes what he's walked into, he groans, "Oh, no." That's how I felt when Ayub led us into the carpet store. No restaurant, just a carpet store. The great Moroccan cliché. And the hit men lying in wait.

Abdellatif suddenly appeared behind us. "Have you eaten yet?" he asked.

I shook my head.

"That's good because we have camel meat," he said. "Small camel. Fresh, very fresh."

He ushered us upstairs, and for a moment I hoped I'd misread the situation. All doubt vanished when I saw the breakfast nook: the end of a long, narrow, windowless room filled with expensive, hand-woven carpets.

We were joined by Aziz, the guy we were headed to all along—the closer. He and Abdellatif spoke Arabic, although both are fluent in English. Andrea and I felt caged, a pair of pigeons nibbling camel meat. Abdellatif ate quickly and departed, his job apparently done.

Another man entered and unrolled carpets as Aziz started his pitch.

"We didn't come here to buy a carpet," Andrea said.

"Nobody does, madam," Aziz said, smiling. "It's always love at first sight."

I mentally replayed our encounter with Abdellatif on the train. He said he'd been away from Marrakech three days, but he carried no luggage. The conductor checked the ticket of every passenger in the compartment but his, as if he had been seated elsewhere. When I asked about the government program, he was vague. It wasn't a leap to now conclude he had been trolling the train for suckers.

My only surprise was that the elaborate ruse left me feeling more disappointed than duped.

The helper kept unrolling carpets as Aziz continued his rap: "Don't worry about price, I make you a good deal…A thousand years guaranteed, I wish you a long and happy life to use it…I don't want to push you, I want to encourage you…"

We were led downstairs, where more helpers unrolled more carpets.

"This one?" Aziz asked Andrea.

"No, thank you," Andrea said, arms crossed.

Aziz waved a dismissive hand at the helper. Another helper rolled out a new carpet over the old one.

"This one?" Aziz said.

"No, thank you," Andrea said.

The pile of carpets grew taller.

"We have a dog," Andrea said. "She's eaten every carpet we've ever had."

"No! No!" Aziz said. "This is Moroccan carpet. They don't eat. A lion could not eat this carpet."

Aziz shared something in Arabic with the helpers, and they laughed. He explained that it was strange that we lived under the same roof as a dog.

The carpets kept coming.

"No more," Andrea said, "it's getting confusing."

"Don't be confused," Aziz said. "Go for them all!"

I looked at the exit—and the six or so men who stood in our way—and wondered how we'd ever get out.

"If you don't buy carpet in Morocco, there will be regret," Aziz said. "Because we do not come to Morocco everyday. Look at this one, madam. This is a painting, this one."

If Andrea even glanced at a carpet, Aziz ordered it set aside.

Amid the flurry of colors and designs, a red wool number caught her eye.

"I complement your taste, madam," Aziz said. "Close your eyes, imagine it back home. Maybe one day I want to go to America to see my carpet in your house."

"How much?" Andrea said.

"I make you friendly price, two thousand," Aziz said. "The price of the year because business is slow."

Abdellatif had reappeared. "Strike while the iron is hot," he said. "When the iron is not hot, you cannot strike."

Andrea might buy a $2,000 carpet, but not without comparing prices and checking our room dimensions at home. She said she would think about it.

Aziz insisted on putting the carpet on hold for her. He told her to return even if she didn't want it, so he could sell it. Andrea said if a buyer wanted it, let it go; she needed time.

"How much time?" Abdellatif said. "We'll wait for you."

"I don't know," Andrea said. "Maybe tomorrow or the day after."

"You have all day to think about it," Abdellatif said. "Why not come back this evening."

"If you want to sell the rug, that's fine," Andrea said.

"We said we would set it aside," Abdellatif snapped. "We're honest. I don't know if you are, but we're honest."

Andrea turned away.

"What do you mean?" I asked Abdellatif, hoping his English had momentarily failed him.

"I mean that we're honest," he said, "and I don't know if she is, if she is honest."

Abdellatif slumped in a chair. He tapped his foot, looking sullen. I was stunned at how badly this train ride had turned out.

The room grew uncomfortably silent. Aziz looked embarrassed. He handed Andrea his business card and said she was welcome back, even if she didn't want to buy anything.

I thanked Abdellatif for the camel meat, but he ignored me. I guess Friday couscous was out of the question.

We left and hired a boy to lead us out of the souk.

We returned the next day to officially refuse a carpet we never wanted.

By then I was grappling with the meaning of the whole sorry episode. It stings to think you're too cynical, then learn you're not cynical enough. I could see my experience with Abdellatif as an isolated incident, or I could see it as one of the dark truths of travel.

Instead, I simply swept it under the rug.

Castles in the Sand, Carpets in a Cave

MERZOUGA, Morocco — The high beams of our rental car poked holes in the blackness and found nothing. The dirt road was rutted and washboard-ribbed; it paralleled and crisscrossed other unpaved tracks stretching into the void. We were heading southeast, 30 miles from the Algerian frontier. Somewhere on our left was Erg Chebbi, Morocco's only expanse of Saharan sand dunes. We could not see where we were, but we were where we wanted to be.

At home, Andrea and I enjoy visits to the desert. We're drawn to the harsh but beautiful landscape, the vast emptiness and the things that fill it. So we were glad to tour the more desolate reaches of central Morocco, meandering 600 miles by car and camel.

We started in Marrakech, driving through the High Atlas, pine-swathed mountains that top 13,000 feet. A week later, crossing over a pass farther north, we'd get caught in a September snowstorm. But on this bright, sunny day we had a clear shot at the mesmerizing wasteland below. We wended through barren auburn hills studded with red-earth casbahs, fortress-like dwellings. We'd entered the domain of the

Berbers, the indigenous people of North Africa who are fiercely independent yet uncommonly hospitable.

That afternoon, outside a dusty speck on the map called Amerzgane, we were stopped at a police roadblock for speeding. An officer handed Andrea's international driver's license to the chief, who sat behind a table in the shade of a palm tree. We braced for a shakedown.

"Do you have money?" the chief asked Andrea.

"I don't know," she said, stalling.

"OK, you can go," he said, waving us on with a smile.

We left the main road and climbed hairpin turns through the Dades Gorge, a narrow red-walled canyon cut into the High Atlas by the Dades River. We stopped at a quiet inn for lunch. After a tomato and cucumber salad, olive omelet, warm bread and melon, our waiter, Mohammed, showed us his home—a small cave. We weren't surprised to see it stocked with wool carpets, as common in Morocco as souvenir T-shirts, and after two weeks here we finally bought one. Our lack of cash was no problem; the cave took plastic.

Our arrival in Agdz made it a one-car town. We sipped cold drinks at a sleepy sidewalk cafe as youths faced off on an ancient Foosball-style arcade table. The proprietor indulged my interest in music, popping tapes into his boombox, settling on one that sounded like 1930s American folk music. It was Izenzaren, a Berber group that uses tambourine, drums and the banjo-like *loutar*. I paid the man 30 *dirham* ($2.75) for the cassette, our theme music for the rest of the road trip.

South of Agdz, in the Drâa Valley, we came upon one of the more striking desert vistas I've seen. Purple mesas towered in the distance, contrasting with a sea of green palms in the foreground. Old casbahs melted into the ground like sand castles claimed by high tide. Children and their elders along the roadside waved at us so benevolently and persistently that we felt as if we were riding in a parade.

In the oasis of Zagora, a billboard painting of a desert scene indicates it's 52 days by camel across the Sahara to Timbuktu. At the open-air market, men haggled over goats whose legs were bound by palm fronds. Buyers lifted the animals' lips to inspect their teeth and gums. One satisfied customer left in a taxi, a pair of goats lashed to the luggage rack.

It was not until the morning, after our arrival near the small village of Merzouga, that we saw how close we'd driven to Erg Chebbi in the dark the night before. About 100 yards from the hotel patio, the immense dunes appeared as sculpted blond mountains.

We needed supplies for an overnight camel trek. A hotel worker showed us to a store, which happened to be next door to the home of his cousin, the rug merchant. We succumbed to the offer of mint tea, knowing where it would lead.

Ahda Achabo, owner of Depot Nomade, said the bold red and royal blue lamb's-wool carpet Andrea coveted cost $800. Andrea countered with $200, and I sighed at the thought of lots more tea.

In Moroccan carpet negotiations, there is "good price," "friendly price" and "last price." To these, Achabo added "nearly my last price." He and Andrea handed pad and pen back and forth, jotting figures until Andrea held firm at $400.

"She is worse than a Berber woman," Achabo joked. "She wants a camel for the price of a sheep." Then he shook on it.

Late in the day, we joined seven Europeans atop camels and ambled into the dunes, our heads wrapped in scarves to protect against sun and wind. Multilingual Berber guides picked a route through shifting sands that changed color from brass to copper with the setting sun. After 90 minutes, ample time for our bottoms to discover the pointy end of a camel's hump, we stopped near a palm patch at the base of a dune taller than a minaret.

Dinner was served under a tent. We ate the *tajine* (thick stew) in the traditional way, with our hands. Our hosts placed our sleeping mats outside.

I crawled under a blanket and drifted toward the sandman. In a dream, a faint voice called to me, "Turn around, turn around." I awoke and, rolling onto my back, beheld the brilliant starry sky. The camp was silent, not even the camels stirred, and for the first time in a long time, I heard my heart.

A Case of Hair Today, Shorn Tomorrow

FES, Morocco — I miss my family, my friends, my dog. I also miss Shannon Weeks.

Shannon cuts my hair. When I'm home, I see her every five weeks at Ralph's Hair Place in the Hillcrest district of San Diego. I didn't fully appreciate her until I left on this journey without learning to say "Just a trim" in multiple languages. If Shannon had been cutting my hair these past months, I'd still resemble someone my mother recognized rather than a survivor of an industrial accident.

You can travel the world for a year without visits to the doctor and dentist. But unless you want to look like Jeff Daniels in *Dumb and Dumber*, there's no avoiding the barber. You'll likely end up in the chair of a man with a sharp glint in his eye and a pair of dull scissors in his hand, as I have many times on this trip. The upside is that it's usually cheap. It also gets you close to an authentic cultural experience—sometimes too close.

In Nepal, the barbers also act as quasi-chiropractors and massage therapists. I wandered into a one-plywood-chair shop in Pokhara, the kingdom's second-largest city, and heard several loud pops as the barber swiftly rotated a customer's head, cracking his neck. When it came my turn, the young barber meticulously snipped away for 45 minutes, giving me the best haircut of the journey. I waved off the spinal manipulation. Looking wounded, he launched into a neck-and-shoulders massage.

He motioned for me to lean forward in the chair and rest my head on my folded arms atop the counter. Before long, he had my shirt hiked over my head. I hadn't seen the previous customer in this position, so I figured the barber was giving me extra massage time in lieu of a neck adjustment. I closed my eyes.

When I opened them, I saw the curtain in the doorway had been drawn, preventing anyone from seeing in. I grew ever more tense as the massage headed south. I bolted from the chair, paid the man and left. Call me culturally insensitive, but he was the only barber to ever put his hands down my pants.

In Ho Chi Minh City, Vietnam, I had my hair cut by possibly the oldest barber in Southeast Asia. He had to be 85, but I'm bad with ages, so he could have been 100. He had a chair in his family's tailor shop. When a seamstress yelled to let him know that he had a customer, it took him five minutes to descend the ladder from his loft.

He was a stooped, frail man who had to turn away often to unleash a deep, phlegmy cough.

The haircut was an ordeal, and I wondered if it might go faster if I knelt on the floor and gave the barber the chair. I shuddered and said "no" when he pulled open an antique straight razor with his shaking hands. He resumed with the scissors, giving me my 70 cents' worth.

His work didn't look bad in front, but I could tell he'd cut skin-close in back. It was 90 degrees outside, and when I hit the street my head felt cold.

The haircuts I got in New Zealand, Bali and England were uneventful. No incense, lotions or rituals—almost like home.

By the time Andrea and I reached Morocco, I was pretty shaggy. In Marrakech, I bargained for my haircut. The barber, a teenager, wanted $6. I offered $2, and we settled at $4. I knew it was too much, but I was paying for the atmosphere. His shop was on the main square, where snake charmers coaxed cobras from baskets and a man walked barefoot across broken glass.

I got careless and dozed in the chair. Andrea, back from shopping in the souk, woke me with a guffaw. The barber had clipped me nearly bald, leaving a pancake-sized patch of hair in front. I now had a buzz cut with bangs, the wackiest 'do I've sported since my grandfather gave me a Mohawk in second grade.

After a week's trip through the desert, we arrived in Fes, where I made the mistake of glancing in a mirror. I looked as though I were growing a goatee on my head. I asked Andrea to crop the patch, but her only scissors were for fingernails, and the scissors for sale in the market were the blunt-edged kind you use in kindergarten.

I searched the crooked streets of the medina until I found a barbershop open on Friday, the Islamic day of prayer. I used sign language to show the barber I wanted my patch clipped.

But he started on the shorter hair, apparently thinking I desired the patch accentuated.

I gesticulated wildly, to the growing confusion of the barber and his partner, who worked on another customer. At last the partner grasped what I wanted, and the two barbers swapped heads mid-cut. The new guy had me shorn down to an even butch in no time.

It was still technically summer, so I called it my summer cut—good for this summer and next.

I'll be glad to get back to San Diego and Shannon. I just hope I'll have something left for her to work with.

Part Six:

South America

Winging From Morocco to Chile, Passing Through Strange Territory... Dallas

SANTIAGO, Chile — We took off in a fog and landed in a daze.

Casablanca was socked in when Andrea and I left North Africa for South America. It was clear here in the Chilean capital when we arrived two days later, but we were far from clearheaded.

We'd made the last big leap of our journey. We were back in our neighborhood, within a few time zones of it anyway. It took only five flights to five countries on four continents—a disorienting marathon through the hyper-stressful world of airports and airplanes. The upside is that we had each earned 12,000 frequent-flier miles, not that we're eager to use them.

Flying within Morocco from Casablanca to Tangier and continuing on to Malaga, Spain, then to London, Dallas and Santiago is like driving from L.A. to Phoenix by way of Boise, Idaho. Our routing was funny, but so is the airline industry. It's usually cheaper to fly round trip than one way. Our problem is that we want to finish in California, not Morocco.

To save money, we flew from Morocco to London (with a connection through Spain), then searched for a round-trip flight to Santiago that stops in the U.S. We found one at a London ticket discounter. When our return flight from Chile to London lands in Dallas in December, we'll collect our bags, skip the connecting flight to London and fly to San Diego on the outbound part of another set of round-trip tickets. I know, it's confusing to me too.

Once I'd left Morocco, I was dragging, and I suffered language lag. At the airport in Malaga I was still saying *shukran*, thank you in Arabic. In England that night, I'd switched to *gracias*. In Dallas, I kept my mouth shut.

Flying in and out of London can get tricky because there are five airports. We landed at Luton, north of the city, and flew out of Gatwick, to the south. Rather than waste time and money on trains, buses and taxis, we drove to our hotel in a rented car we dropped at Gatwick the next day.

At the Skylane Hotel, near Gatwick, two drunken men stumbled down the hall, bellowing about a non-existent karaoke bar. A sign welcomed those attending a psychic fair, but I didn't need a psychic to tell me this long-haul trip would get weirder.

At the Dallas-Fort Worth airport, we went through Immigration so we could wander around rather than wait in the transit lounge. Andrea worried we might break our rhythm by entering the U.S. before journey's end. But after 10 months abroad, the States felt like another foreign country.

We stepped outside and slammed into a hot and humid Texas night. There was the smell of fried food in the air, and grease practically dripped from the sky.

After spending much of the past year in the developing world, everything about America seemed big. Big cars, big luggage, big people, big talk.

"I just put a home theater in my house," I heard a man say. "Oh, man, is it big!"

My mission in Dallas was to mail our request for absentee ballots for the upcoming election. (We asked that they be sent to us in Bolivia, where we plan to arrive in time to fill them out.) It might have been easier to fly back and vote in person. You can buy postcards every 20 feet in the airport, but good luck getting a stamp. I found a lone stamp machine at the end of the huge terminal. It took exact change, no bills. The smallest packet of stamps cost $2; I didn't have a single coin.

After separate purchases of paperbacks, newspapers, mints and Q-Tips, I had eight quarters. Before I returned to the stamp machine, I stopped in a boarding area to address the envelope. A flight attendant sat behind me, dumping her boyfriend over a cellphone. In my haste to give her some privacy, I jumped up, sending the coins in my lap rolling across the floor. The woman probably wondered why I was crawling around at her feet, but she continued the breakup. Call me insensitive, but I've never missed an election. I found seven quarters and gave up on the eighth when the woman told the guy she would always love him.

I hate asking for change. Cashiers act as though you're robbing them. So I bought a bottle of water I didn't want.

With tax, it came to $1.99, leaving me 24 cents short. I finally asked another cashier to break a dollar. He caught my crazed look and handed me the coins. I'll vote for whomever promises easier access to postage.

The overnight flight to Chile was brutal. I know air rage is a problem, but it's a wonder there isn't more. It's not natural to hurtle through the sky in a metal tube for hours on end with 300 tightly packed strangers.

Jet lag, fatigue and giddiness made me want to gnaw on my floatation device. I dozed in a half-sleep, which is worse than no sleep. When I woke, my eyes stung and it felt like a 747 had landed on my neck.

The view out the window made it all worth it. The sun was rising over the snow-covered Andes. It was spring in the Southern Hemisphere.

When we walked off the plane, the air was crisp and invigorating. After flying for two days, it was finally time to travel.

A Chilean Ramble
Long on Beauty and Hospitality

COPIAPÓ, Chile — To travel without expectation is to invite surprise.

Andrea and I arrived in South America largely ignorant of Chile, having scarcely cracked our guidebook. The lack of a rough itinerary was not by design. The longer we wander, the less time there is to plan. So we came prepared to see only what was put in our lazy path. Lucky for us, Chile picked up the slack.

Joined by Andrea's mom, Phyllis, of San Diego, we left the capital, Santiago, in a rental car and meandered mainly north during the next week for 500 miles. It felt like a lot of ground, but we merely covered the waist of this long, skinny country that stretches about the same distance as Los Angeles to Anchorage. Still, it was far enough to be dazzled by some of Chile's rugged coast, vast desert, lush vineyards and soaring mountains.

We spent the first night in Las Cruces, a resort town on a small, sandy bay midway down the Chilean coast. Most of the vacation homes were buttoned up, awaiting summer in the Southern Hemisphere. Packs of handsome, well-behaved dogs roamed everywhere—in the streets, on the beach, inside the church. We were the only guests at the Hotel Villa Trouville, where the Pacific Ocean slammed against the rocky point below our window.

In the morning, we drove a few miles north to the hamlet of Isla Negra to tour the former seaside home of Pablo Neruda, one of Chile's two Nobel laureates in literature. The snaking, quirky house is built like a ship, with round ceilings and narrow passages. It's crammed with marvelous objects the poet collected during his wide travels as a government diplomat— carved ships' figureheads, African masks, glass piano casters, crucifixes, a life-size wooden horse.

Two days later we reached Zapallar, a tony coastal village an hour north of Valparaíso. Modern villas and old mansions spill down a hillside of pine and cypress trees to a crescent of white sand. We sipped drinks in the sun at an empty cafe as fishermen mended nets and flying pelicans surveyed the clear, blue water.

When the Pan-American Highway briefly left the coast, the snow-capped Andes, out of sight for the last three days, suddenly leapt up before us. Men, buffeted by the wind, sold rounds of goat cheese on the side of the road.

In La Serena, Chile's second oldest city after Santiago, Andrea and Phyllis headed for La Recova handicrafts market, where they bought baby alpaca sweaters, handmade copper boxes and lapis lazuli jewelry.

Later in the week, we left the main route and headed inland to the pleasant town of Vicuña. The region is the site of international astronomical observatories because of the exceptional clarity of the northern Chilean sky. We climbed stairs to the dome of the Cerro Mamalluca observatory and peered through a telescope at galaxies, clusters and nebulae. When I glimpsed 100,000 stars in a speck of space where my naked eye had seen nothing a moment earlier, our trip around the world suddenly felt like a weekend jaunt.

The next day we drove farther east, up into the Elqui Valley, an area thick with vineyards of muscat grapes. The distilled wine produces the brandy called pisco, the Chilean national drink. The green vines, along with the purple petals of blooming jacaranda trees, contrasted brilliantly with the brown mountains rising from the valley floor.

Back on the main road, we continued north through the Norte Chico, the semiarid zone between the fertile heartland and the barren Atacama Desert. The region is usually an expanse of bleak scrubland, but we caught it during the rare phenomenon known as *desierto florido* (flowering desert). Every four to eight years, heavy winter rains prompt dormant seeds and bulbs to sprout through September and October. As we sped along, we saw dull shrubs standing amid vibrant carpets of wildflowers—purple, yellow, red and blue.

In the small city of Copiapó, we settled into Hotel la Casona, a quaint inn with pastel walls, Diego Rivera prints and down quilts. It was our last and favorite in a series of charming, family-run hotels in this clean, affordable and friendly country.

We hired Sebastián Martínez, a local mining student, to take us in his four-wheel-drive pickup to the striking, desolate plateau between the two ranges of the Andes. We drove 100 miles east on a bumpy dirt road that climbed through mountains streaked with copper, iron and sulfur. After crossing a 13,000-foot pass that left us lightheaded, we descended to Laguna Santa Rosa. Dozens of pink flamingos waded in the green, salt lake. A guanaco, a wild relative of the llama, gazed down from a knoll. A fox timidly approached us as Sebastián tossed bread crumbs. It was easy to squeeze off a couple of rolls of film.

We continued around the lake, no one else in sight, passing the ruins of an Incan settlement studded with bits of pottery. We returned over a different pass. An hour later, an approaching cloud of dust heralded the only other vehicle we saw that day. It was a Brink's armored truck, bound for a mine at nearby La Coipa to pick up a load of gold bars. The cargo it would carry back down the mountain was like the landscape we'd gaped at all week: precious.

Discovering the 'Wow' Factor
On Bolivia's Plains

UYUNI, Bolivia — We were in northern Chile when our driver pointed to the smooth black asphalt rolling east. "That's the road to Argentina," he said. He suddenly turned north onto a rutted piste. "This is the road to Bolivia."

Andrea and I chuckled nervously, wondering what we'd signed on for, but awe soon replaced apprehension. For three days we bounced over the Bolivian Altiplano, the high, treeless plain stretching between the two ranges of the Andes. The magical 300-mile journey through the remote region gave us the sensation of leaving the planet. By the time we finished in this desert city 275 miles south of La Paz, I'd said "wow" so often my lips were cracked.

A length of pipe atop two metal posts guarded the Bolivian border crossing. Waiting on the other side with a four-wheel-drive Toyota Land Cruiser were Roberto, our guide, and his wife, Wilda, our cook. After we were grouped with three European travelers, Roberto made up his own road across the vast plain, flanked by volcanoes, Dali-esque rock formations and mineral-stained mountains. Sulfur spilled down like yellow rivers, flowing onto a basin the colors of coffee, chocolate and cinnamon.

A cloud of steam marked the Sol de Mañana geyser patch. We carefully picked our way among the bubbling mud pots, heat radiating through our shoes, flecks of boiling earth splashing our pants. One geyser roared like a jet engine, and I strained to hear Roberto say, "One of these could go off at any minute." I stopped playing Innocents Abroad and headed for the truck.

We passed flamingo-dotted salt lakes, none more spectacular than Laguna Colorada, where microorganisms dye the water red. The rare James' flamingos that feed on algae are a vibrant red and pink. They appear as bathers in a sea of blood that laps a snow-white borax shore.

The scenery was not all that took our breath away. We had topped 16,404 feet—nearly 2,000 feet higher than Mt. Whitney—and felt the effects of the thin air. Roberto and Wilda offered us coca tea, the Bolivian cure-all, but we five gringos rode out the night on water and aspirin. None of us could fall asleep in the wind-lashed bunkhouse. The energy it took to roll over made me gasp for air. My head throbbed, and my eyes ached. I was better but still a little disoriented in the morning. When I tried to brush my teeth, I missed and brushed my chin.

The second day took us closer to Andean wildlife. Vizcachas, relatives of the chinchilla, bounded over red volcanic slabs. When we tossed bread to the long-eared, furry rodents, they shared it with mice. Llamas grazed on spongy grass, as did vicuñas, their smaller, wild cousins. That night

Wilda served llama meat. From the viewfinder to the frying pan. I didn't have the heart to help myself to seconds.

We rose early the third day to watch the sun rise on Salar de Uyuni, the largest salt flat in the world, about 100 times bigger than Utah's Bonneville Salt Flats. The blinding white remnants of a prehistoric salt lake stretch so far and wide, you can see the curve of Earth. We felt we were in the Arctic until we reached Isla de Incawuasi, a cactus-covered island standing in the ocean of salt. The island, home to a Bolivian couple, their dog and an eagle named Álberto, boasts cacti 30 feet tall and 1,500 years old.

Back in the truck, we streaked across the salt pan. Hexagonal ridges formed by the sun tattooed the white crust, so the world now looked like a giant soccer ball. Indeed, the trip was a kick.

A Brief Pause for Prison in La Paz

LA PAZ, Bolivia — William Aponte, my tour guide, was waiting. He has plenty of time these days. Ten years, to be exact.

That's how long a judge gave him for drug trafficking. He's serving his sentence at San Pedro Prison, across from the Plaza Sucre in downtown La Paz. San Pedro's convicts pay their own expenses. Aponte leads tours to get by. Anyone with 51 *bolivianos* (about $8) and a twisted sense of adventure can see his home.

San Pedro is a notorious prison. The 1,500 inmates run it. The cells are apartments that lock only from the inside. When an inmate's time is up, he sells his unit and furnishings to the highest bidder. Convicts buy and cook their own food or eat in restaurants run by other prisoners. Those with money live well; those without subsist on bread and watery soup and sleep outside.

Tours are unofficial. There are no ticket windows or postcard stands. After I agreed to Aponte's fee through the bars of the front gate, he made eye contact with a guard who let me in. Aponte would later pay the guard 40 *bolivianos* and split the rest with a robber named Romeo, the prison enforcer, a burly man who followed me for my protection and perhaps to ensure that I paid.

The gate clanged behind, and I stood in a courtyard thick with murderers, rapists and thieves. Andrea stayed behind, ready to call whomever you alert when a Bolivian prison tour goes bad.

I shook hands with Aponte, 42, the father of three. He wore a clean polo shirt, jeans and a gold watch. He was caught at La Paz airport trying to sneak 11 pounds of cocaine onto a flight to Switzerland. He grinned as I kept swiveling my head, looking for anyone who might harm me. "Don't worry," he said. "No problem."

I followed Aponte through a maze of dark passages that emptied onto connecting patios surrounded by two-story buildings. Inmates sat behind piles of potatoes, carrots and onions. Others sold canned goods, cigarettes and toiletries from tiny stores. A convict clipped hair in his barbershop, and a few doors down, a fellow inmate shot portraits in his photo studio. Prisoners ate lunch under red umbrellas emblazoned with the Coca-Cola logo. One vendor poured fruit smoothies from a blender. Two inmate-doctors staffed a for-profit clinic; one is in for drugs, the other for murdering his wife.

Accommodation in the convent-turned-prison ranges from hovels that sell for a one-time fee of $200 to penthouses that fetch $3,500 when vacated. I did not see it, but Aponte said one rich drug dealer had contractors outfit his flat with a sauna.

We stepped over a few penniless inmates sleeping on a balcony to reach Romeo's room, which had a refrigerator, stove and microwave oven. In his bedroom loft were a double bed, color TV, VCR and PlayStation computer games. The Righteous Brothers' "Unchained Melody" came from the CD player.

"This is like a small town inside a big city," Aponte said. "If you have money, you can have anything you want here." That includes liquor, prostitutes, weapons, even a band to perform at your birthday party.

Many of Aponte's "tourists" are people buying drugs. One inmate offered to sell me 10 grams of pure cocaine for $100. Guards don't search visitors coming or going. They rarely enter the prison. Their job is to keep inmates from escaping— and to take a cut of all contraband that passes under their noses.

The prison's town-like look is made all the more real by the presence of children. About 100 kids live with their fathers; the number swells at Christmas and Easter. Many of the children attend a nearby school, returning to the prison in the afternoon to play on a patch of asphalt. Aponte insisted no one dares touch the kids, but on New Year's Eve 1997, a girl was raped and murdered.

Aponte led me farther into the rambling complex. Peruvian terrorists played cards and watched TV outside. Younger inmates shot pool for money in a billiards hall decorated with pinup girls. A man sold ice cream from a freezer. A bartender poured beer and whiskey.

"The time goes fast here," Aponte said.

After I left, I sat across the street in the park and wondered what to make of the tourist site. What a strange world, I thought. The old woman next to me must have read my mind. She threw her head back and laughed.

On Lake Titicaca, Listening for Incas, Hearing the Whispers of Childhood

COPACABANA, Bolivia — I first heard the name Lake Titicaca in my sixth-grade geography class. Once the snickering stopped, most of us thought it would be a cool place to visit. After 32 years, I went to see for myself.

It wasn't hard to find. Andrea and I hopped a northbound bus in La Paz, and three hours later we stood on the shore of the lake that legend claims gave birth to the Incas and the sun. Straddling the border of Bolivia and Peru at 12,500 feet, it's one of the highest navigable lakes in the world. Some say it evokes the Mediterranean, but with the snow-covered Andes in back, that's a stretch.

I expected to see indigenous people crossing the lake in dugout canoes. Instead I found Indians renting paddleboats on the beach, steps from a kiddie merry-go-round. What would the Incas say?

Our hotel, La Cúpula, was more attractive, if less authentic. Run by a German and Egyptian couple, the white-domed inn stands on a hillside of eucalyptus overlooking this dusty town and the blue lake. We liked the abstract painting in our room so much, we bought it. In the round restaurant with wrought-iron seat backs resembling Picasso figures, we ate pink filets from trout the size of barracuda.

On the Plaza 2 de Febrero, cars, trucks and buses lined up in front of the Moorish-style cathedral, waiting to be blessed by a priest wearing a baseball cap. Women in bowler hats and ruffled skirts sold garlands, ribbons, wreaths and other vehicular ornaments. The priest sprinkled holy water on the engines and on the heads of drivers and passengers, praying for a safe journey. Following tradition, travelers toasted themselves before dousing tires and bumpers with beer and champagne. The ritual seemed counterproductive when one bus driver downed six glasses of beer and climbed behind the wheel.

In the morning, we boarded a double-decker boat for Isla del Sol (Island of the Sun), where it's said the first Inca emperor, Manco Capac, and his sister-wife, Mama Ocllo, mystically appeared. The lake was an angry sea, with whitecaps and rolling swells. Our boat was named Titicaca, a comfort when I saw that several other boats lurching on the water were christened Titanic.

In the village of Cha'llapampa, a local stopped his soccer game to open the Isla Museo for us. The tiny museum contains medallions, vases, puma-faced incense burners and other artifacts of the pre-Inca Tiahuanaco culture recovered 25 feet underwater. A trail climbed past mud houses up the mountain to a rock slab thought to have been used by Incas for human and animal sacrifices. Nearby, the labyrinthine Chincana Ruins crumbled above a crystal bay.

We hiked seven miles along the island's spine, terraced fields tumbling to the lake on either side. Women tilled the dull ground, children at their hips. We passed cattle, sheep, pigs, a dog with the head of a German shepherd and the body of a basset hound.

The trail ended at the Escalera del Inca (Inca Stairway) and Fuente del Inca (Inca Springs), where natural spring water spills down channels along ancient stone steps. Spanish explorers thought they had discovered the fountain of youth. Today, at the bottom of the stairs, Indians sell Cokes and Pringles, and girls pose with llamas for money.

I wanted to take the first boat back to the mainland, but the captain made us wait for the second. I was miffed until I saw I now had time to skip rocks across the water, something I would have done had my sixth-grade class come here on a field trip. Trouble was, the Incas long ago skipped all the best rocks on Lake Titicaca. Still, after 32 years, it was good to finally put a place with the name.

Fear and Trembling on the Road?
You Bet Your Life

BERMEJO, Bolivia — I could pummel the bus driver.

Andrea and I are careening down a muddy mountain road. Our bus has bald tires, bad brakes and a driver out to prove Charles Darwin wrong.

Nothing slows him down. Not the night fog, the blind curves, the construction detours that jump up at the last second. As he cuts corners, I feel the right rear tire leaving the narrow road. If the front one joins it, we'll plunge from a cliff hundreds of feet above the Rio Bermejo. I can already hear the screams.

We're sitting in two of the front passenger seats, and the view through the windshield is like a scene from a horror film. We're riding from Tarija, in southern Bolivia, to the town of Bermejo, on the Argentine border. The 105-mile trip can take anywhere from six hours to a lifetime.

Here's the dirty little secret of travel in less wealthy nations: You often entrust your life to someone you might not trust to watch your luggage. Your perception of risk is warped. You worry about disease, violence and terrorism, but what you should truly fear is any man with a wheel in his hands.

More than 1 million people worldwide die each year in road accidents, most in developing countries, according to the World Health Organization. The Association for Safe International Road Travel tells me my chances of dying on the road abroad can be 20 to 70 times higher than in the U.S. It's a growing problem. By 2020, a Harvard School of Public Health study predicts, road accidents will be the planet's third leading health burden.

I was vaguely aware of these sobering statistics when we left last January, but not overly concerned. I was a vagabond then, heading for adventure. I'm a superstitious short-timer now, heading for suburbia. My new goal is to return safely to America, where I can stop fretting about buses, taxis and rickshaws and resume worrying about guns.

So what are we doing in this speeding sardine tin? No choice. The transportation dollar goes a long way in poor countries, but it doesn't buy safety. Competition drives bus tickets down to pennies a mile, leaving little extra for brake fluid. Whatever you spend, you'll travel poorly constructed, poorly maintained and poorly lighted roads, with poorly paid and poorly trained drivers who flout the poorly enforced traffic laws. And when the inevitable occurs, you'll wait to be rescued by the poorly funded or nonexistent emergency medical team.

Flying is the obvious alternative, but you miss the sights. Besides, down here they have these pointy things that poke the sky called the Andes. Bolivian aviation gets dicier on the ground. We watched a jet try to land at the Sucre airport only to see it roar off at the last instant when the pilot spotted dogs on the runway. Departure taxes apparently don't cover the cost of a fence.

I'm not averse to risk in travel. In 1994 I went skiing in Sarajevo, Bosnia-Herzegovina, during the war. Later that year I crossed the U.S. without money. Had I died during these arguably foolish journeys, at least it would have been in the pursuit of unique thrills. That's more than you can say for a bus crash, which is a mundane, needless, pathetic way to go. If this bus driver kills me tonight, I will surely die again of embarrassment.

Safety may be a luxury in some countries, but caution is free. I understand everyone has a right to a living, even if it's hauling passengers down gnarly roads in deathmobiles. But with equipment and conditions stacked against them, I don't get why many drivers ignore the one thing they can control—their own driving habits.

After nearly a year of traveling, I've noticed a paradox: the slower a country's pace of life, the more reckless its drivers. In many places we've visited, motorists are the only people moving with any sense of urgency. I want the travel agent to hurry, not the bus driver.

Our young bus driver stops at a roadside cafe. After the break, he returns with a teenage girl who rides shotgun. Our scary bus trip has turned into a first date. The bus driver pops tapes in and out of the cassette player while eating and chatting up the girl. He's trying hard to impress her. At least he won't fall asleep. I just hope there isn't one of those tragedies that brings young lovers closer.

The driver makes change with one hand and steers with the other. His urge to pass every vehicle in front of him is as primal as thirst, hunger, sex. We fishtail around each curve, sliding ever closer to the black edge of the precipice.

I could pummel the bus driver. But I don't. This is the guy I've entrusted with my life.

Packing Tips for a World Tour: Mind Your Socks, Forget Bandanna

BUENOS AIRES — Here's my maxim for packing: The longer the trip, the lighter the luggage. That stuffed super-sized Samsonite may fly for the weekend wedding in Indiana, but try hefting it on a crowded, moving bus in Indonesia.

I've traveled most of the year with a 15-pound backpack. It's so light I don't use the shoulder straps and instead carry it like a briefcase. Andrea has the same model pack but with more in it. Her zipper broke three continents ago, and she can now beat me at arm wrestling.

I didn't know how light I was traveling until we came here to the Argentine capital from Bolivia. We had tickets to the ballet at the grand Teatro Colón, and I emptied my pack in a futile search for evening wear. Rather than panic, I employed my maxim for attending the theater dressed as a rube: Arrive late, leave early; we all look the same in the dark.

When roaming the world for a year, you can look smart or you can pack smart, but you can't do both.

Some tips:

No matter how little you lay out, it won't fit in your luggage. Compression is the key. Like most things in life, clothes are mostly air. Place garments in a special plastic bag with one-way valves. (Eagle Creek's Pack-It Compressor and Space Bag's Travel Genie are two such items.) After you stomp the air out, your wardrobe will be reduced to a manageable wad that looks like shrink-wrapped food.

With this method, you'll want clothes made of a crammable fabric. Most of us don't wake up and say "I love the feel of synthetics in the morning," but there's a reason this stuff was invented. My two polyester shirts and one pair of nylon pants have been beaten on laundering rocks from Bali to Bolivia, and they still hold their creases. I just steer clear of open fires.

Andrea's fabric of choice is silk. It's lightweight, and wrinkles fall out easily. Her silk skirt and blouses have kept her cool in hot countries where it's offensive to wear shorts and tank tops.

Hanging toiletry bags are critical. They're organized and fold nicely, and you can always find a place to hang them, even if only a doorknob. Why not bring your standard toiletry bag and set it on the bathroom counter? What counter?

You can't have too many locks. We sleep better on trains knowing our packs are secured to luggage racks with a stretch cable lock. A combination Master Lock was handy in India, where many budget hotel room doors close with unlocked latches. We fasten the zippers on our packs with luggage locks. When you travel with only one spare shirt, you guard it like the Hope Diamond.

Other useful yet light gear: a silk sleep sack, for beds with grotty (or no) sheets; waterproof bags to keep medicines and documents dry while your pack rides on a bus roof in the rain; self-adhesive tabs, to mark pages in guidebooks; a calculator, for figuring prices in other currencies; a disc-shaped rubber sink stopper (many hotel sinks don't have plugs), so you can do laundry; and, yes, an inflatable hanger.

I'd literally be lost without my key ring compass. I wouldn't trust it for orienteering in the woods, but it's great for navigating cities. When I got turned around in the narrow, twisting alleys of Varanasi, India, I recalled that the Ganges was east and my hotel was on the river. All I had to do was keep one eye on the "E" of my compass while keeping the other on the cow dung at me feet.

There's a lot of bad packing advice out there. Among the so-called essential items I've found useless are a cup, spoon, sarong and bandanna. If you're visiting places where you need your own cup and spoon, you're wandering a different planet than I am. A sarong, a wraparound piece of clothing that doubles as a beach towel, is ideal for a rave on a Thai island, but there's no need to hump one through the Himalayas. I lived 42 years before I bought a bandanna, and I wince each time I see it in my pack. Maybe we'll hit a dude ranch on the way home.

Aside from a passport and money, the only essential items for a long journey are outstanding socks. Not good socks, not great socks, but $20 non-itching, non-chafing, moisture-wicking, wool-nylon-Lycra-blend socks. They'll protect your feet, last forever and not embarrass you too badly between washings. They may not get you the best seat at the theater, but $20 socks will carry you a long way in this world.

No Doom, No Gloom—
Just Friendly Folks
At the End of the World

USHUAIA, Argentina — There's a bowling alley at the end of the world. A movie theater too. Casinos, ice cream parlors, sporting goods stores, ATMs, Internet cafes, restaurants that serve whiskey and homemade chocolate. The end of the world has it all.

Argentines call this harbor town of 44,000 the end of the world because it's the southernmost city on the planet. They don't care that several Chilean islands and Antarctica lie farther south. How many stuffed penguins emblazoned with *El Fin del Mundo* (The End of the World) do they sell in Antarctica?

To reach the end of the world, you head south out of Buenos Aires on Route 3 and follow it until the pavement and ferries stop 2,010 miles later. Or you can fly, as Andrea and I did. We came to see what the end of the world looks like.

It sits at the bottom of Isla Grande, the biggest island of Tierra del Fuego, the Argentine-Chilean archipelago cut off from the South American mainland by the Strait of Magellan. The town is wedged between the north shore of the Beagle Channel, named for the boat that brought naturalist Charles

Darwin here in the 1830s, and jagged glacial peaks that leap from the sea. Mt. Olivia looms in the distance like the Matterhorn's evil twin. The land is not as harsh as it sounds. Red and yellow tulips grow in front of City Hall.

A good first stop on a tour of the end of the world is the End of the World Museum, where the staff will stamp your passport to prove that you experienced Ushuaia's claim to fame. Artifacts show the life of the region's earlier inhabitants, nomadic Yahgan Indians who traveled by canoe and kept their naked bodies warm with sea lion fat. A few blocks away, the Maritime Museum displays ship models and recounts the building's years (1902 to 1947) as a prison.

One morning I joined seven other passengers aboard the Tres Marías, a small excursion boat that cruises the Beagle Channel. After passing out lollipops, skipper Héctor Monsalve motored us to Isla de los Lobos, where a dozen sea lions sunned on the rocks. At nearby Isla Alicia, hundreds of black-and-white king cormorants sat atop nests of seaweed and guano.

Monsalve later cut the engine and donned a wetsuit and diving gear. He jumped into the 45-degree sea with a waterproof video camera. We watched on a closed-circuit TV in the cabin as he aimed the camera at the crabs and sponges below. When Monsalve resurfaced with two king crabs for us to inspect on the deck, I asked whether he was going to throw them back in the water.

"In the water, yes," he said, smiling. "But in a pot of boiling water."

Twenty minutes later, the group feasted on fresh crab, French bread and white wine.

Many tour buses make it to the end of the world. Most wind up at Tierra del Fuego National Park, a 155,000-acre spread of lakes, rivers and glaciers along the Chilean border. Andrea and I marched past the crowds into a forest thick with beech trees. We followed a coastal trail along the Bahia Lapataia and, passing steamer ducks and kelp geese, we soon had the end of the world to ourselves.

They are mighty hospitable at the end of the world. When Julius Linares, owner of Residencia Linares, heard our bus left at 5:30 a.m., he insisted on rising to fix us breakfast.

"I have to give you your farewell," he said.

In the morning, after coffee and biscuits, he called a taxi and saw us to the street.

"Muchas gracias," I said. *"Adiós."*

"Ciao," Linares said.

Yes, they say *ciao* at the end of the world.

Ending With an Appetite
For a Few Last Discoveries

PUERTO MONTT, Chile — They say that when traveling through southern Chile, where transportation is notoriously unreliable, you always know when you'll leave but you never know when you'll arrive. Only the second part is true. But at least it's a gorgeous spot to sit and wait.

As our wander year approached the end, Andrea and I had two weeks to get from the bottom of South America to this port city, where we made plans for our return to San Diego. It's a 1,000-mile trip as the crow flies, but we saw no crows in Chilean Patagonia. We instead followed a twisting, backtracking route, relying on buses, ferries, planes and minivans that run at three times: late, really late and tomorrow. But along the way, we glimpsed some of the most stunning scenery of the journey, gaping at pristine fjords, glacial peaks and dense native forests.

We left Ushuaia, the southernmost city in Argentina and the so-called end of the world, and traversed Tierra del Fuego by bus before crossing the Strait of Magellan on a ferry. After Ferdinand Magellan discovered this passage that links the Atlantic and Pacific oceans, his men were afraid to sail back through it. No wonder, the wind can blow you to New Zealand.

In the Chilean city of Punta Arenas, we wandered through the magnificent cemetery, where sculpted cypress trees flank the extravagant tombs of the founding fathers. Most lavish is the tomb of wool baron José Menéndez, who rests in a replica of Rome's memorial to Vittorio Emanuele II.

West of the city, we toured the Seno Otway Penguin Sanctuary, where 3,000 Magellanic penguins return every year to nest. The monogamous birds reclaim the same burrows each pair occupied the year before. We watched from beachside blinds as penguins waddled single file from the sea. Down the road, protected gray foxes and ostrich-like nandus meandered in the tall, waving grass.

A six-hour bus ride north took us to the spectacular Torres del Paine National Park, where dramatic granite spires jut from the Patagonian steppe. Andean condors circled above, and austral parakeets darted below as we hiked trails flanked by glacier-fed lakes, fire-red notro flowers and herds of llama-like guanaco.

Torres del Paine was also where we encountered the highest concentration of Chile's leading import: wind.

The road north through Chile ends at the park, so we returned to Punta Arenas and hopped a flight to Balmaceda, 440 miles south of Puerto Montt. That put us on the Carretera Austral (Southern Highway), a largely unpaved 600-mile track cut into a wilderness of temperate rain forests, cascading rivers and snowcapped mountains.

Transportation through this region is sporadic at best. A daylong van ride became all the more arduous when an intoxicated passenger soiled himself early in the trip. Windows were rolled down and noses were held, but the stench was overpowering. One fellow backpacker who could not take it bolted from the van and flagged down a semi-truck headed in the opposite direction.

At the misnamed Puyuhuapi Channel (it's a fjord), we crossed by boat to Termas de Puyuhuapi, an unpretentiously elegant wood-and-glass lodge set on a lonely peninsula crowned by lush peaks. The stress from our transportation woes melted away as we soaked in the thermal pools fronting the ice-blue fjord.

A bus that was eight hours late delivered us to the seaside town of Chaitén, where we met Nicolas La Penna, a guide who gives free music lessons to local youths. Some 12-year-old uniformed schoolboys dropped by La Penna's house at lunchtime, and an impromptu jam session ensued in the front yard. La Penna dashed in and out of his house to retrieve ever more guitars made of native wood, and the boys played folk, rock, country and blues while holding schoolbooks between their knees. So we weren't left out, La Penna hung large drums around our necks, and we tried to keep a beat.

In the morning, La Penna drove us north to Parque Pumalín, the largest privately held conservation area in the world. Funded by American millionaire Douglas Tomkins, the park covers nearly 750,000 acres, stretching from the Argentine border to the Pacific Ocean.

A footpath wended through the virgin temperate rain forest, leading us to a wooden suspension bridge spanning a clear stream. On the other side, we gazed up at towering alerce trees, some as many as 4,000 years old. Our rustic and impeccably furnished cabin was built of reclaimed wood and looked out on sea lions fishing in Renihue Fjord.

This stunning setting was also where we were ambushed by the Unarians, pseudo-religious UFO cultists. There were four of them: two American women and a Chilean couple with a 40-year age difference who couldn't keep their hands off each other. The Unarians were annoying, clingy and creepy.

The six of us were the only guests at the resort. And since staff saw us arrive in the same van, they assumed we were together. They put us in adjacent cabins and sat us at the same table for every meal. The female Unarian leader preached about past lives and outer space while the Chilean couple kept sucking face. When they pushed their holy book on me, I gladly accepted, figuring that time spent in my cabin reading would be time spent out of their orbit.

But there was no escaping the Unarians.

La Penna returned for all of us two days later and drove us back to Chaitén. I groaned when I learned that the next ferry north wasn't for another 12 hours. Chaitén wasn't big enough to hold the Unarians and us.

Andrea and I managed to give the Unarians the slip, checking into a dive motel for the day. Our plan was to hide out until we all had to board the ferry. By then it would be late at night, and the Unarians just might go to sleep.

We entered our room. It was dingy and cramped, but it was peaceful. For about an hour.

There was a bellowing out in the street. The Unarian leader was hollering our names. "Mike and Andrea!" she kept screaming, louder and louder. We tried to ignore her, but she wouldn't let up. We feared she intended to conduct a door-to-door search of Chaitén until she found us. She finally guilted us out of our hideaway.

The four Unarians had located a private plane and pilot. They asked if we'd split the cost of the flight to Puerto Montt. No thanks, we said. The last thing we wanted was to share an aircraft with a bunch of kooks anxious to hook up with extraterrestrials.

We thought that was the end of it. But the Unarians decided to bag the plane and wait for the ferry—in our room. I wanted to cry. They crowded onto the bed, where they remained the rest of the day, talking UFOs and making out.

The overnight ferry from Chaitén to Puerto Montt arrived a respectable five hours late. After we disembarked, we fled from the dock, hoping to escape the Unarians. But Andrea wasn't fast enough. They caught her and offered us a ride into town. It was a long way to our hotel, and I could tell Andrea wanted the ride. I ignored the discussion and kept running, figuring Andrea would take the hint.

She called to me. I refused to stop. If Andrea wanted to hang with the Unarians, so be it.

Andrea yelled at me. I turned around and yelled back.

And just like that, the Wander Year had logged its first fight.

We had come so far. Nearly 12 months around the world, and not a single spat. Now a perfectly good record had been blown to bits and carried off on the nerve-fraying Chilean winds.

Well, screw the Unarians and the spaceship they rode in on!

I checked into the hotel and closed the curtains. When Andrea turned up, I looked over her shoulder to make sure she wasn't followed. There was only one choice. We laughed and laughed and quickly made up. Why let some tiresome Martian-loving zealots ruin the trip of a lifetime?

There were one or two close calls in the days to come—the odd, heart-stopping Unarian sighting—but we managed to keep our heads down and melt into the city.

We rented a car. We had a few days left. We would use them to visit the glorious Lake District, where emerald waters sparkled beneath fairy-tale mountains. But this leg of the trip would feel more like a vacation than the continuation of a journey.

The journey had ended here in Puerto Montt. It was hard to believe, but our year of wandering was over. Now it was time to start the long trek home. Like the penguins, we were sure to remember the way.

Part Seven:

Home

The End of the Road

SAN DIEGO — We were thrilled to reach our latest destination. Our Spanish-style accommodations offered a comfy bed, large towels, plenty of hot water and a fireplace. It should have felt familiar. We were home, after all.

Or were we?

The address was the same one my girlfriend, Andrea, and I left last January when we flew to Fiji to start our trip around the world. But now that we had completed the circle a year later with our arrival from Chile, the front door of our house opened to another foreign place. The light switches were not where I reached for them. The doorknobs seemed lower. When I left phone messages, I couldn't recall our home number.

Our pets, cared for the past year by the fellow who rented the house, had swapped personalities. Aretha, the cat, who usually greets our return with a shoulder cold enough to frost a beer mug, was positively giddy. Maya, our shepherd mix, would leap into the lap of a dogcatcher, but when we rushed through the gate, crying her name, she yawned and turned her back. We thought of her every day of our journey, often gazing at the photos of her we attached to our luggage tags, and now she didn't know who we were.

But there were aspects of our return that weren't so bad. It was divine to shuck the nylon travel pants I wore nearly every day for a year and step into some jeans. I marveled at how cars stopped for me at crosswalks. I enjoyed the heft of a full-size bar of soap, rather than the puny cakes that squirted from my hands in budget hotel showers from Bangkok to Buenos Aires.

After visiting 22 countries in the South Pacific, Asia, the Indian subcontinent, Europe, North Africa and South America, our wander year is over, and we are overwhelmed.

We're happy to catch up with family and friends, but our return to the U.S. leaves us displaced. We are refugees of a sort, caught between a dream world that was the experience of a lifetime and a real world that we have yet to redefine.

Andrea was 40 and I was 42 when we decided to enjoy today what we might not be around to enjoy tomorrow. We had no children or other obligations to hold us back. We had traveled before but never for as long. With a few exceptions, we chose countries we had not previously visited. That we didn't get everywhere on our wish list—Turkey and Kyrgyzstan, among other destinations—only means a future itinerary is already taking shape.

There are some years when so much life happens you can't live it all at the time it occurs, and this was one of them. I'm sure that decades from now, we will flash on profound and poignant moments we're still to realize from this trip. It will take awhile to grasp the lessons we've learned and the changes we've experienced. And although we may not know the meaning of it all yet, we can look back on the obvious.

We are lucky, and we know it. For a year, we woke each day with the sole mission of getting dressed and trotting the globe. When we think of 2000, we'll say: "That's the year we traveled around the world. We started the millennium in style."

Postcards are lovely, but there is no substitute for laying your eyes on nature's wonders in person. I had no idea that parts of the world are so staggeringly beautiful. We did not spot a single blemish in New Zealand, where it's hard to tell where the pristine national parks end and the rest of the country begins. I've wondered what the west coast of North America looked like 100 years ago, and we may have glimpsed it in southern Chile, where neither people nor buildings block your view of virgin forests, crystal streams and majestic mountains.

The contrast between the green oases and the purple mesas of the Drâa Valley in southwest Morocco are so brilliant that we had to squint behind our shades. In Halong Bay, Vietnam, we sailed among 3,000 lush limestone islands that rise from the emerald water like jade steeples. A ride across the surreal landscape of the Bolivian Altiplano delivered us to bubbling mud pots, rainbow colored peaks, gleaming salt flats and pink flamingos. I know there are rivers that flow with toxic waste, skies that are choked with smog and rain forests that fall to bulldozers, but it's still a pretty planet.

There is more to travel than scenery. We found the whole package in the magical kingdom of Nepal, where the lofty spirit of the people matches the grandeur of the Himalayas. "Don't try to change Nepal; let Nepal change you," the saying goes, and it did. We were humbled to see life simply lived, inspired by souls who meet the burdens of the day with a smile. *"Namaste,"* they say in greeting to anyone in their path, which means loosely, "I salute the god within you."

Travel challenges your assumptions. Information now spreads at the speed of light, but it's still possible to venture into the world badly misinformed. Listen only to the sound bites that make the news, and it's easy to picture China as a grim country of 1 billion oppressed, a threat to global stability and a potential enemy. So we were surprised when Darth Vader didn't meet us at the airport. Sure, China has its problems, but far from miserable, most of the people we saw appeared genuinely content. I had to question my belief in the universal appeal of our economic and political values. I'm as patriotic as the next guy, but if our system is best for everyone, why do we call it the American Way?

Aside from some of the most striking landscape of the journey, we found in China a hospitable people who had more in common with us than we knew. In the southwestern province of Yunnan, we were the only foreigners on a modern Mercedes bus that showed a subtitled video of *My Best Friend's Wedding* while driving a new freeway between Lijiang and Kunming. When we stopped at a roadside cafe, we shared pork, fish, eggplant and rice from a revolving tray with eight other passengers. No one spoke to us, so I assumed there was a language barrier or that they resented us.

When I dumped some red sauce on my food, a young woman said in English, "That's spicy." I laughed and wondered how often I'd mistaken shyness for indifference. The others smiled and started chatting with us in English. They were business professionals on vacation. When they learned we were Americans, they were eager to hear what we thought of their country. They asked where we had been and suggested other stops. They were proud of China and wanted us to have a good time. Our governments may disagree, but these people did not feel like my enemy.

Besides revealing the fundamental similarities of people around the world, travel can expose us to our fascinating differences. I struggled as a tourist in India, but these many months later, I recall it as the most compelling country of our journey.

In the sacred city of Varanasi, we hired a boatman to row us on the Ganges at sunrise. Hindus, who believe in reincarnation, hold that dying in Varanasi and having one's ashes scattered on the holy river guarantees the soul release from the cycle of rebirth. When our boat pulled in front of the burning ghat—the riverside steps where the dead were being cremated in open fires—I was at once repulsed and riveted. The boatman inexplicably rowed ashore, where eight shrouded bodies burned simultaneously on separate heaps of wood. Workers held scarves to their mouths and tended the pyres with sticks while others carried baskets of ashes atop their heads to the holy river. The flames warmed our faces, and the sweet smell of sandalwood powder sprinkled on the bodies filled our nostrils. A stack of bamboo poles yanked from the stretchers used to carry the dead sat near the water. The boatman picked through them, searching for the makings of a new oar. As male relatives of the deceased circled the bodies in a ritual, I never felt as conspicuous in my life.

But I suddenly saw that nobody noticed us, and the funerals went on amid a hubbub of activity. Children leaped into the water from steps next to boats laden with wood for the pyres. Women in saris and men in loincloths bathed in the river, while others brushed their teeth or washed clothes. Pilgrims prayed and meditated. Cows munched on the dry grass used to kindle the fires. When a cricket ball rolled down the steps of the burning ghat, a boy did not hesitate to retrieve it. A scene that had looked bizarre now appeared natural. Life and death blended on the river in harmony. As we floated away, I realized that it may be a crowded planet, but there's ample room for a multitude of lifestyles and beliefs.

You can learn a lot about your country by leaving it. I used to think most criticism of America sprang from jealousy, but now I believe it's born of bafflement. Many around the world see us as work-obsessed, materialistic, gun-loving and zealous. Like all generalizations, it's an exaggeration. But it was bliss to go a year without hearing the phrase "dot-com" or looking at people who appear to have grown cellphones from their heads.

We were constantly reminded of our impact as tourists. You can follow the adage to "take only photos, leave only footprints," yet still leave giant footprints. Banana pancakes and Bob Marley tunes, staples of the backpacker diet, are served worldwide, often to the exclusion of local fare. In Bali, Indonesia, young men have abandoned the family rice fields to drive taxis; now traffic and congestion strangle an island fewer are calling paradise. Coca-Cola is sold outside the ancient temples of Angkor, Cambodia, and seemingly everywhere else in the world. Some women of the Andes have learned they can make more money posing for snapshots with a llama than by weaving the animal's wool. I don't know the answer, but I'm troubled that my application for a passport can unleash a chain of unintended consequences.

We made some mistakes. One I made repeatedly was my habit of regarding strangers with suspicion. Reeling from the relentless sales pitches in India, I waved off most anyone who approached me the rest of the trip. I avoided hassles, but no telling how many interesting conversations I denied myself. Most touts, hawkers and wannabe guides are harmless. Besides, people after your money can be the most entertaining of all.

One of the things we did right was to pace ourselves. After some tough miles in Southeast Asia, we flew from Malaysia to Scotland and rested in one of our favorite places in a rented flat. Spanish school in Ávila, Spain, let us linger in one picturesque spot for two weeks. And visits by friends and relatives in New Zealand, Ireland, Spain and Chile revived our spirits along the way.

Andrea and I relied on each other a lot. People are amazed we traveled together for a year, virtually 24 hours a day, with only one little squabble. The strain of prolonged travel tests a relationship, and we earned an A. It was easy.

We might have met more people had we roamed alone, but traveling as a couple let us do things we might not otherwise have tried. I never would have attended the symphony in Hanoi, the ballet in Madrid and a jazz concert in La Paz, Bolivia, without Andrea's prodding. Andrea would have skipped the British Open golf championship had I not been along. And together we discovered our new passion of trekking. We learned why New Zealand's Milford Track, with its towering waterfalls and glacially carved valleys, is called "the finest walk in the world." The 104-mile Cotswold Way afforded glorious views of the western English countryside. If there is a postcard of heaven, it might resemble the trailside vista in Chomrong, Nepal, of the mystical peaks Annapurna South, Machhapuchhare and Hiunchuli.

It's a young world. It was refreshing to watch children amuse themselves without expensive high-tech toys and video games. My heart soared when Indonesian kids shouted with joy as their kites made of plastic trash bags danced on the wind. In Patan, Nepal, boys excitedly played table tennis on a crumbling slab of cement, using a line of bricks for the net.

It's an unfair world. We can't choose our parents. Where we're born is a cosmic crapshoot. Americans, even the poorest among us, are born with advantages most others will never know. Don't leave these shores if you can't face how good you've got it. You'll find almost unimaginable poverty and suffering, endured by people who never had a choice. Every day I was forced to admit, there but for sheer, dumb luck go I.

Despite its cruelties and atrocities, it can be a benevolent world. We encountered a level of civility and respect Americans rarely extend to one another. Nothing bad happened. We weren't assaulted or pickpocketed. Nothing was ever taken from our rooms. We've returned without a scratch, let alone a single hurt feeling.

The cost of our journey was $51,470—about a third higher than our original budget. We may be foraging for food next month, but we'll have no regrets.

Our modest goal when we left was to take a break. That now sounds naive. A break implies that you will resume a routine. While I continued work as a writer, Andrea quit a good job in the health insurance industry. The immediate future is uncertain. Even if we had routines to step back into, this enriching year would have altered our view of them. For us, a new journey begins in an unfamiliar place called home.

A few days after we got back, Maya, our dog, seemed to remember us. Or maybe she just likes the new people who have moved into her house. I continued to feel unsettled. After the simplicity of living out of a 15-pound backpack in hotels for a year, there were now too many choices: too many shirts, too many shoes, too many rooms to enter.

I found myself pacing. I kept stopping in front of the globe we had left a year ago on the kitchen counter. That's how our wander year started. A couple of spins and a dream. The globe spoke, and we listened. A year later, I've returned to end the conversation:

Thank you, World.

The Wander Year by Numbers

Continents visited: 6

Countries visited: 22

Times across the equator: 6

Flights: 45

Beds slept in: 169 (plus one sand dune)

Total cost of trip: $51,470

Air transportation: $12,816

Ground transportation: $6,428

Lodging: $12,938

Food and beverage: $9,285

Tours, excursions: $3,283

Gifts, souvenirs: $2,243

Shipping gifts and souvenirs home: $516

Internet charges: $570

Newspapers, books, magazines: $734

Laundry: $114

Bowling (twice in China): $9

Miscellaneous: $2,534

Most expensive dinner for two: $104, Blue Lobster Restaurant, Singapore

Least expensive dinner for two: $2.50, Alka Hotel, Varanasi, India

Most expensive hotel: $149, Hosteria Las Torres, Torres del Paine National Park, Chile

Least expensive hotel: $1, Purnima Guest House, Shika, Nepal.

Afterword

It's 11 years on and I've yet to regain all the weight I lost in New Zealand. Andrea always said that my best feature was my plump posterior, but that never grew back. She didn't hold it against me, though. In 2005, after living together for a decade, we were married. We're well into a new streak of harmony: no squabbles since Puerto Montt. Of course, we've steered clear of the Unarians.

Our wander year recharged Andrea, and she resumed her successful career, thriving in her new field of employee wellness. I continued to write travel and golf articles, and later moved to fiction. I recently published my first mystery and have started on the next.

We still live in the same house in San Diego, though some of the occupants have changed. In 2007, at the age of 18, Aretha moved on to that great litter box in the sky. "Life didn't cheat her," our vet said. He said the same thing a year later when he also had to put down Maya, who nearly made it to 13. Last Thanksgiving, we brought Olive, a little tortie cat, home from the pound. She plays fetch, so she doubles as our dog.

We've continued to travel, though nothing on the scale of 2000. Limited to periodic vacations, we've pursued our passion for links golf, making many trips to play the coastal courses of Great Britain and Ireland. In between, we've also enjoyed jaunts to Canada, France, Italy, South Africa and Japan.

As I predicted, our journey has come to mean more to us with the passage of time. With the exception of a penniless trek I made across America, our wander year is the most memorable time in my life, an extended period of feeling intensely attuned and engaged. Andrea feels the same.

We are reminded daily of our grand tour by the mementos that fill our house: paintings from India, antique tribal hats from China, Buddhist statues from Nepal, Balinese placemats, Vietnamese carvings, Moroccan rugs. Hanging in our bathroom is a framed series of photos that depict two pilgrims trekking through the Himalayas, boys playing in Fiji and a group of men sitting against a church door in La Paz, Bolivia. Not a morning passes that I don't stare at their pictures and wonder how these fellows are doing.

But it's the mental snapshots of people and places we encountered on our magical year that remain the most vivid. The high priest from the Jain temple in Ranakpur, India— "I'm a very busy man..."—frequently pops into my head; I Googled him the other day and there he was, right down to those brown socks. I can still smell the sandalwood from the burning ghat on the Ganges River in Varanasi. I can still feel my bony butt bouncing in the back of that four-wheel-drive as we crossed the Bolivian Altiplano. And even though I never met her, I often think of Jenny Xu.

The backpacks we used in 2000 now rest on a shelf in my office. Sometimes I'll pull mine down, unzip the compartments, and marvel at how I lived most of the year with only 15 pounds of luggage. Tucked away in some drawer is Andrea's inflatable hanger, now gasping for air.

After we returned, we moved the globe from the kitchen counter back into the den. It has sat on an end table in a corner of the room, largely ignored. Some years, I haven't even looked at it. But recently, it keeps catching my eye. It even occasionally draws me near.

Someday, we hope to reach for the globe and give it another spin.

San Diego, California
July 8, 2011

Thank You

Thank you for reading *The Wander Year*. I'd be grateful if you'd take the time to share your opinion of it with other readers at Amazon.com and Goodreads.com, or wherever you go to discuss books.

Also, if you'd like to get an email when I publish my next book, please sign up here: http://eepurl.com/Jl_gn

Many thanks!
Mike McIntyre

About the Author

Mike McIntyre is an author, journalist and traveler. His journeys have taken him to more than eighty countries. He has worked as a travel columnist for the *Los Angeles Times*, a theater columnist for the *Washington Post*, and a feature writer for the *San Diego Union-Tribune* and the *Budapest Sun*. He's also published articles in *Golf Digest*, *Reader's Digest*, *Air & Space/Smithsonian* and *Powder* magazines. When not traveling, he lives in San Diego.

Also by Mike McIntyre

The Distance Between: A Travel Memoir

The new travel memoir from the bestselling author of *The Kindness of Strangers* and *The Wander Year*...

In his most personal book yet, lifelong vagabond Mike McIntyre invites readers into his little corner of the world—a corner that is always moving. As a young man, McIntyre careened around the globe to escape boredom, bad jobs and a broken heart. Over the next three decades, he instead journeyed the world to encounter challenges, captivating characters and valuable life lessons. In this collection of forty-six stories from twenty countries—including such far-flung locales as Guatemala, Hungary, Bhutan, Sri Lanka, China and the United States—McIntyre traverses the distance between traveling to escape and traveling to encounter. Humorous, heartfelt and unflinchingly honest, *The Distance Between* finds McIntyre at the peak of his narrative powers, and once again affirms why the *Los Angeles Times* calls him "a superb writer."

The Kindness of Strangers: Penniless Across America

The #1 Amazon Travel Bestseller.

As featured on Oprah, *The Kindness of Strangers* is the story of one man's continental leap of faith—and the country that caught him.

Stuck in a job he no longer found fulfilling, journalist Mike McIntyre felt his life was quickly passing him by. So one day he hit the road to trek from one end of the country to the other with little more than the clothes on his back and without a single penny in his pocket. Through his travels, he found varying degrees of kindness in strangers from all walks of life—and discovered more about people and values and life on the road in America than he'd ever thought possible. The gifts of food and shelter he received along the way were outweighed only by the touching gifts of the heart—the willingness of many he met to welcome a lonely stranger into their homes…and the discovery that sometimes those who give the most are the ones with the least to spare.

The Scavenger's Daughter: A Tyler West Mystery

Disgraced newsman Tyler West is desperate for a scoop that will save his career. When he investigates the baffling deaths of several of San Diego's elite, he uncovers a common link: torture devices not used since the Dark Ages. Plunged into a mysterious world of medieval torture scholars, antiquities collectors and sadomasochists, he must break the brilliantly conceived series of slayings that has cast a dark shadow over a city better known for its sun, sand and surf. The elusive killer goes by the name Friar Tom, in tribute to his hero, Tomás de Torquemada, the first Grand Inquisitor of the Spanish Inquisition. As Ty scrambles to unmask the monstrous zealot, he is drawn into a lethal game of cat and mouse that could cost him everything.

CPSIA information can be obtained at www.ICGtesting.com
Printed in the USA
LVOW12s0006251114

415364LV00005B/894/P